Tracing Marco Polo's China Route

Wang Miao & Shi Baoxiu
Photographer: Wang Miao

CHINA
INTERCONTINENTAL
PRESS

图书在版编目（CIP）

与马可·波罗同行／王苗，石宝琇著．—北京：五洲传播出版社，2004.9
ISBN 7-5085-0602-2

I. 与 ...　II.①王 ... ②石 ...　III.
游记－作品集－中国－当代－英文　IV. I267.4

中国版本图书馆 CIP 数据核字 (2004) 第 105169 号

与马可·波罗同行

策　　划：北京凤凰华文传媒顾问公司
撰　　文：王　苗　石宝琇
摄　　影：王　苗（除图下署名外）
责任编辑：张　宏
装帧设计：田　林　傅晓斌
封面绘画：文中言
制　　作：北京原色印象文化艺术中心
承 印 者：北京恒智彩印有限公司
出版发行：五洲传播出版社
　　　　　（北京北三环中路 31 号 邮编：100088)
开　　本：787×1096(毫米)1/16
字　　数：120 千字
印　　张：13
版　　次：2004 年 9 月第 1 版
印　　次：2004 年 9 月第 1 次
书　　号：ISBN 7-5085-0602-2/I·43
定　　价：72.00 元

CONTENTS

Preface

The story of Marco Polo's journey across the vast land of China has entertained and informed generations of people all over the world since it was first published nearly 700 years ago. Being exploration enthusiasts, we had long indulged in the romantic dream of one day identifying and tracing Marco Polo's route through northern China.

Marco Polo chose the most perilous route possible from Venice to China, a country still shrouded in mystery and myth in the Western world. His incredible adventures in Asia and the book he wrote made this Italian merchant world-famous. Upon its publication, *The Travels of Marco Polo* created a furore throughout Europe, and is still widely consulted today.

In the sections related to China, Marco Polo described in vivid detail the society, people, customs, local products and important events existing in China during the Yuan Dynasty (1271-1368). However, not being a guidebook, it does not give any account of the specific route the traveller took, measuring distances by how many days it took to go from one place to the next. This deficiency was exactly what we so desperately needed in order to plan our journey.

Thanks to Prof. Li Han of Wuhan University, who provided us with many useful materials, and Prof. Yang Zhijiu, an expert on Marco Polo at Nankai University

in Tianjin, we managed to piece together enough information to follow his route.

Nevertheless, today it is physically impossible to completely follow in the steps of Marco Polo, because over the past 700 years the topography in this part of the world has changed a great deal. Due to the southerly movement of the deserts and the fact that many rivers have changed course, his original route has long since disappeared and a new one has come into existence.

For these reasons, we could only approximately trace Marco Polo's route, a route which he traversed by horse and camel, while we had the modern comfort of a car. On a mid-summer day we began our journey by jeep from Kunjirap Pass in the Pamir Highland.

left: A Qing-Dynasty scroll "The Snow-Coved Tianshan".

top: A Yuan-Dynasty blue and white porcelain vase.

bottom: The Tang-Dynasty tri-coloured glazed pottery figurine with the motif of the camel carrying the musicians shows the prosperous and merry scene on the then Silk Road.

Travelling eastward we passed through Xinjiang, Qinghai, Gansu, Ningxia, Inner Mongolia and Hebei. When we arrived at our final destination of Beijing, it was autumn and yellow leaves carpeted the ground.

Our 12,000-kilometre route started from a

plateau over 4,000 metres above sea level and ended in the North China Plain at an altitude of less than 100 metres. Along the way we met Tajiks, Uigurs, Yugurs, Tus, Huis, Mongols and Hans, observed their life styles, and saw the different scenery each region has to offer.

Covering such a long distance in only 80 days was no easy task, even with today's excellent

communication and travel facilities. It is hard to
imagine the difficulties Marco Polo faced 700 years
ago making a journey of over 5,000 kilometres
without the modern conveniences that we now all

Today, the people living in Xinjiang still travelling on the ancient Silk Road on the antique means of transportation.

take for granted. However, through his book we are afforded a glimpse into what it must have been like in those days, and his travelogue remains an important and unique historical document. More than that, it

Wuwei is a major town on the Hexi Corridor and is famous for the local "Heaven Horse." The bronze statue named "Horse Stepping on the Flying Swallow" unearthed here has been a Chinese tourist token. This is the city token "Horse Stepping on the Flying Swallow" which is towering in the city.(Photo by Xie Guanghui)

Suoyang City in Anxi. It was the seat of Guazhou in Tang Dynasty, the city wall is grandiose.(Photo by Shi Baoxin)

Marco Polo traversed numerous mountains and rivers and finally reach the interior of China.

The enchanting scenery of
Selim Lake.

provides would-be adventurers like ourselves with inspiration and motivation to continue the task that he began.

A abandoned antique castle on the Masar-tagh Mountain which is abrupt in the Taklimakan Dersert.

DID MARCO POLO REALLY VISIT CHINA?

I n human history, 700 years is not a great length of time, however an enormous amount of changes can occur over seven centuries. In the 13th century when Marco Polo made his historic trip to China, both communications and transportation were extremely basic, with none of today's technology, and contact between nations was minimal. People in the West had heard wild stories about Orientals – a race of short people with "yellow" skin. And to people in the East, Westerners were known only as being "barbarians" with red hair and green eyes. It was in this climate of ignorance and misunderstanding that the three Polos set out for the East.

There can be no doubt that Marco Polo was an extraordinary man. Not only did he travel beyond the conventional boundaries for European travellers of that time, he also lived as a foreigner in China for 17 years under the protection of the Great Kublai Khan. As if this were not remarkable enough, upon his return to his own country he was promptly put into prison, where he wrote *The Travels*, a book that would change the course of history forever.

Three and a Half Years *En Route* to the Yuan Capital

Let us first take a brief look at Marco Polo himself before we follow his travel route into China. Marco Polo was born into a merchant family in Venice in 1254. His father Nicolo Polo and uncle Mafo Polo were both merchants, doing trade as far

as the Volga River in Russia. It was said the two brothers had once been to China.

In 1271, 17-year-old Marco Polo joined his father and uncle on their voyage to the east to look for broader trade markets. This time their destination was the prosperous and powerful Mongol Empire ruled by Kublai Khan. The Polos first took a merchant ship from Venice and landed at Acre on the eastern shore of the Mediterranean. Then by horse, camel and sometimes on foot, they went through Syria, Mesopotamia, Iran, the vast desert in Central Asia, crossed over Pamirs and entered what is today China.

The three travelled by way of Kashi, made a detour at the southern fringe of the Taklimakan Desert, passed through the Hexi Corridor, went through Ningxia and Inner Mongolia, and in 1275 finally arrived at Shang-tu, the Yuan capital, where they paid their respects to the Yuan emperor Kublai Khan. It took them three and a half years to make

The mural painting "Official Document Deliverer" in an ancient tomb in Gansu shows the official document deliverer moving on a horse on the Silk Road.

the entire journey, with stops and detours along the way.

During his 17 years in China, Marco Polo was appointed an official of the imperial government, according to *The Travels*. With this capacity, he travelled all over China and was sent on diplomatic missions to Japan, Burma, Vietnam, Siam, Java, Sumatra and India. If this is all true, Marco Polo was one of the few Europeans to extensively travel throughout China and other Asian countries and leave a written record of his experiences.

The first Chinese translation of *The Travels of Marco Polo* was published in 1913.

An Unexpected Battle Gave Birth to *the Travels*

In 1291, the Polos were at last on their way home when Kublai Khan asked them to join an escort party in charge of delivering a Mongolian princess who was to marry the Persian king. This was their last mission for the Yuan emperor. They boarded at Quanzhou port, sailed via Persia and returned to Venice in 1295, after an absence of more than 20

years.

Back home, Marco Polo began to set up a business in Venice. A war unexpectedly broke out between Venice and Genoa, and he was taken captive in a sea battle while serving as a warship captain in 1298.

The dark Genoese prison was the birthplace of Marco Polo's *The Travels*. There he met Rusticiano, a romance writer from Pisa with whom he shared a cell. With plenty of time on their hands, the two began a collaboration that would astonish the world.

Rusticiano's hand-written copy was quickly

This is the house that belonged to the Polo family. However, after being away for 24 years, upon their return none of the three Polos could even recognize it.

circulated throughout Europe. So much in the book
about the East – its history, geography and culture
– was new to Europeans, and some quite hard to
believe. Paper bill that Chinese started to use as
early as the Tang and Song dynasties, typography
and powder were considered novelties. Coal, not
yet discovered in the West, had been used in China
since the Han Dynasty (206 B.C.-A.D. 220), and the
city of Hangzhou, with its 3,000 bathhouses and
100,000 households was simply unimaginable.

Thus the strange tales related in *The Travels* caused a great sensation in Europe, and although the book was attacked by some as a pack of lies, it still enjoyed great popularity. *The Travels* served as inspiration for both merchants and adventurists, who regarded Asia as a mysterious land full of promise.

It even fired the imagination of no less a person than Christopher Columbus, who treasured his well-thumbed copy. In his diary, Columbus more than once referred to *The Travels* and how the book had given him ideas to plan his eastern expedition. The Portugese adventurists Vasco da Gama and Henrique o Navegador, who discovered India, were also influenced by *The Travels*.

Several Points of Contention Cast Doubt on *the Travels*

In 1477 a German edition – the First printed edition – was published, and by 1929 there were 76 editions in translation. Since publication of *The Travels*, many of the incredible stories related in the book have been confirmed, and it is still widely consulted by scholars. Its value in understanding life during the Yuan Dynasty is unquestionable, but at the same time much controversy has surrounded the book as well. At first the arguments were over the accuracy of its details, however nowadays an even larger question is being considered: did Marco Polo ever actually visit China, or is the book based entirely on hearsay and rumor?

The debate among scholars revolves around

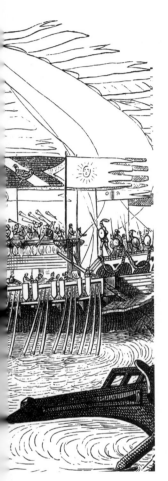

The ship of Marco Polo's time.

top: Shown here is the first printed edition of *The Travels of Marco Polo*, published in German in 1477. On the cover is a drawing of Marco Polo as a youth, with the words, "This is a portrait of the great Venetian traveller Marco Polo, who witnessed many extraordinary wonders of the world never seen before, and recorded them here for posterity."

bottom: A set of Feng Chengjun's three-part edition of *The Travels* is in the collection of Zhongshan University in Guangzhou.

several points of contention. Firstly, if Marco Polo were really so highly regarded by Kublai Khan, and was given a high position as an official in the imperial government, why wasn't his name mentioned in the vast historical records of the Yuan Dynasty? Furthermore, if Marco Polo had really been to China and was familiar with Chinese culture, why did he fail to mention both Chinese tea and Chinese characters – two products typical of Chinese culture – in *The Travels*?

There is also no description of printing – one of China's great inventions, and there are many questionable figures and events which cannot be verified. Marco Polo was even not clear about the family tree of the Mongolian emperors. Lastly, many Chinese place names were spelled in Persian. Why didn't Marco Polo use Chinese spellings if he had really been to China?

The above questions support the arguments of some scholars who believe that Marco Polo never went to China. The early 19th-century German scholar K. D. Hullmann regarded *The Travels* as a mere church legend, a poorly designed travel book for missionaries and merchants.

Scholars Agree That There May Be Inaccuracies

Then in 1979 J. W. Heagei, an American scholar, put forth a new argument. He said that Marco Polo had really been to China, but he only visited the places around Beijing, certainly not as many places as he described in *The Travels*, let alone diplomatic

missions to neighboring Asian countries. Mr.
Heager suggested that Marco Polo probably heard
the stories about other places in China from local
officials who came to the Yuan court. He also
believed that Marco Polo had never become a high
official in his 17 years in China, nor was he highly
regarded by Kublai Khan. He was an attendant of
honour and his job was to go between Beijing and
Kaiping (Shang-tu), take part in hunting and tell
European stories to entertain the Great Khan.

Despite the inaccuracies, most scholars today
accept that Marco Polo did in fact had been to
China. The British scholar Henry Yule, French
scholars Henry Cordier and Paul Pelliot, the
American scholar F. W. Cleaves and the Italian
scholar Leonardo Olschki have been aware for
many years that *The Travels* is not 100 per cent
accurate, but they have all devoted their lives to the
study of Marco Polo and his writings. They have
done thorough research into *The Travels*, consulting
the historical records of Iran and the Mongolian
history, and have concluded that Marco Polo did in
fact travel to China.

Proof That the Polos Were in China Finally Found

Chinese historian Yang Zhijiu, a specialist
in Yuan history, has spent his whole life in the
research of Islamic history and in gathering first-
hand material about Yuan history. In 1941, Professor
Yang found in *The Yong Le Encyclopaedia - Jingshi
Dictionary - Zhanchi* important historical data which

proved that Marco Polo had been to China. The document said that three diplomatic envoys sent to China by the Persian king were returning to their own country, and there was also a note about the grain rations for the three and their companions.

The key point here is the names of the three envoys. It is mentioned in two chapters in *The Travels* that the wife of the Persian king Argon had died and that the king sent three envoys to China to ask Kublai Khan to bestow upon him a new wife of the same nationality as his dead wife. As the three envoys were about to leave for home, the Polos were asked to join the escort party to take Princess Cocachin to Persia by sea. The three envoys in *The Travels* were named Oulatai, Apousca and Coja. Professor Yang found the corresponding Chinese names of the three envoys in *Zhanchi*.

The same event was mentioned in both Chinese and Persian histories, and the names of the envoys were the same as in *The Travels*. This could not be a

Marco Polo died in 1324 in Venice, Italy, leaving behind his last will and testament. Today this piece of paper is considered a treasure by scholars doing research into the life of Marco Polo.

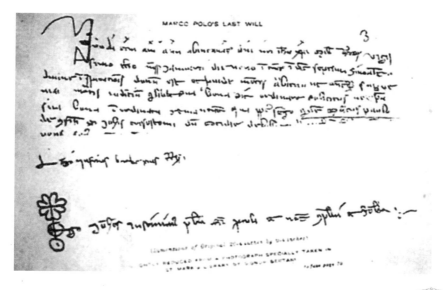

MARCO POLO'S LAST WILL

coincidence. That is to say, though Marco Polo's name was not directly mentioned in the Yuan historical records (very possibly because of his low rank), other important evidence has been found to prove that the Polos left China in 1291. Since their departure was mentioned, there can be no doubt that they were in there.

BEGINNING IN THE PAMIR HIGHLAND

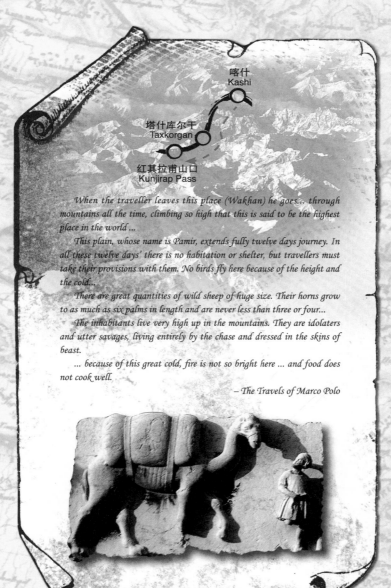

喀什
Kashi

塔什库尔干
Taxkorgan

红其拉甫山口
Kunjirap Pass

When the traveller leaves this place (Wakhan) he goes... through mountains all the time, climbing so high that this is said to be the highest place in the world ...

This plain, whose name is Pamir, extends fully twelve days journey. In all these twelve days' there is no habitation or shelter, but travellers must take their provisions with them. No birds fly here because of the height and the cold...

There are great quantities of wild sheep of huge size. Their horns grow to as much as six palms in length and are never less than three or four...

The inhabitants live very high up in the mountains. They are idolaters and utter savages, living entirely by the chase and dressed in the skins of beast.

... because of this great cold, fire is not so bright here ... and food does not cook well.

– The Travels of Marco Polo

Four of the world's great mountain chains, the Tianshan, Kunlun, Karakorum and Hindu Kush, converge in China's western borders to create the Pamir Highland. It was from here that Marco Polo and his companions first entered the land of China centuries ago.

Now 700 years later at Kunjirap Pass on the Sino-Pakistani border, a thoroughfare leads across the same barren mountains, via which busloads

Pamir Highland is an major passageway of Chinese-Western communication of ancient time.

of Pakistan business people and tourists come into China every day. Travellers today still have to suffer some of the hardships – the cold and the problems due to lack of oxygen – that Marco Polo had to endure, but for only a few hours rather than 12 days.

The barbarous tribes written about by Marco Polo no longer exist. Instead, the area is inhabited by the Tajiks, who follow the Islamic faith. They love to sing and dance and are very hospitable and kind. One similarity with olden days is that they raise the same kind of super-long-horned sheep that Marco Polo once saw.

Along the way, we passed many of the ancient post stations, lakes, rivers and mountains that Marco Polo described in his book *The Travels of Marco Polo*. We also ran into a group of foreigners trying to climb a great mountain peak mentioned by Marco Polo in his book. Coincidentally, they turned out to be from Italy, compatriots of Marco Polo.

Throughout Chinese history, travellers from the Western Regions and India have had to pass through the Pamir Highland. Zhang Qian, an envoy sent by the Han Dynasty (206 B.C.-A.D. 220) to the Western Regions and the famous Buddhist monk Xuan Zang (Tripitaka) of the Tang Dynasty (618-907) both had to surmount this cold and inhospitable highland.

Seven centuries later, we found ourselves following in the footsteps of such venerable explorers, although we had the benefit of a car to take us into the Pamirs. Though it was towards the

As described in Marco Polo's book, the Pamir Highland today is still a barren land and sparsely inhabited. The local Tajik people live in low earthen houses, which provide better shelter against the cold.

The Tajik people, like the
Russians, are descendants
of Europeans, therefore
their features are notably
different from China's other
nationalities.

end of August when we arrived, it felt like autumn on the highland, which is an average of 4,000 metres above sea level.

Along the Gez River, the smooth, asphalt surface of State Highway 314 runs between the capital city of Ürümqi and the bordertown of Taxkorgan on the Chinese side. Occasionally we would see luxurious coaches coming from the Kunjirap Pass, carrying Pakistanis, mostly businessmen, on their way to the

The Kirghiz living on the lower plateau areas look quite different from the Tajiks, both in their facial features and in the way they dress.

city of Kashi.

Brilliant Lakes and Snowy Mountain Scenery

At 7:00 in the evening we came to the banks of Karakuli Lake. The weather was unusually beautiful and the sky a brilliant blue. The lake is extremely deep, fed by water melted from the ice and snow coming down from the mountains. On the other side of the lake stands a solemn, massive mountain called Muztagata. The reflection of the sun on the snow-covered mountain was so bright and it was difficult to open our eyes.

At a height of 7,546 metres above sea level, the peak is one of the tallest in the Kunlun Mountain range. It is crowned with ice and snow that has been accumulating for ages, and just the solid ice alone is estimated to be over 200 metres thick. When the mountain is seen from afar, it appears stately and majestic, but when seen close-up, it

The tomb chambers of the Tajik people are decorated with murals.

is even more impressive. No wonder its name, Muztagata, in the Tajik language means "Father of All Ice Mountains".

Standing by the lake opposite Muztagata is the tallest peak on the Pamir Highland, called the Kongur, rising 7,719 metres above sea level. It too is covered with snow and ice all year round, and the glaciers that move slowly down its slopes send out dazzling lights like cascading waterfalls.

The grassland by the lake was dotted with beautifully-coloured tents, temporary living quarters that the local tourist bureau had prepared for its guests. To sleep by the lake on the highland is without doubt a special experience.

Not far from our tent were five small tents occupied by mountaineers belonging to the Xinjiang Mountaineering Association. They had been there already for three months, and thanks to warm temperatures and good weather, several teams had already made it to the top of the mountain.

A painting with the subject of Zhang Qian's visiting to Western Regions as an envoy.

The Tajiks: Chinese Europeans

The next day we arrived at the county town of Taxkorgan. The only street in town had few pedestrians or animal-driven carts, and motor vehicles were even rarer. Not surprisingly, the town is described as a place where there is "only one street, one light and one loudspeaker, which can be heard all over town".

The Tajiks and Russians are the only two ethnic groups in China that are of European origin, with long, straight noses, deepset brown eyes and black hair. Of the total Chinese Tajik population of over 26,000, more than half make their home in Taxkorgan. At the Tagarma grazing ground, we saw a group of very charming kids with brownish hair, blue eyes and white complexions, the skin colour the Tajiks are born with. As they grow up, their skin will gradually turn a dark red under the highland sunshine. Their habit of kissing each other when they meet is perhaps a vestige of their European cultural heritage.

They call themselves the descendants of eagles, saying that only eagles and the Tajiks can live freely and happily in the harsh conditions of the Pamir Highland. One of their favorite pastimes is the eagle dance, in which they stretch out their arms and flap them as if they are eagles soaring in the sky. Their dance is accompanied by a tune that sounds like eagles crying, played on short flutes made from eagle bones. Very high-pitched and loud, the flute music can travel far and wide on the vast highland.

Calling themselves descendants of the eagle, the Tajiks learn how to do the Eagle Dance at an early age.

Making Our Way Up Kunjirap Pass

Next, we drove west towards Kunjirap Pass. On the banks of the Taxkorgan River we saw a small pagoda built of earth, standing solitary beside the pebble-covered river. We went inside the hollow pagoda, which was about the size of one room. Our guide said that many structures like this could be found around here, but few were as well-preserved as this one. We learned that during the height of the Silk Road, these buildings served as "hotels", or post stations, for merchants and foreign envoys. We

could not help wondering if perhaps Marco Polo had once spent a night in this earth room.

Heading towards this important mountain pass, we could not help thinking about all the ancient caravans that must have travelled in these same steps. When one considers that back then only

the most basic means of transport were available, it is even more astounding that so many made it

On the shores of the Taxkorgan River an ancient post station with a domed roof still stands intact.

through. Apart from cold and hunger, travellers also had to endure complete solitude for up to two weeks at a time, spurred on only by their confidence and conviction in their endeavors,

The bride and bridegroom of
Tajik Nationality.

top: It hardly ever rains on the Pamir Highland, so the roofs of Tajik houses are usually made of tree branches, which allow sunshine to come through.

bottom: The Tajik people are natives of the Pamirs and have been here for generations.

whatever they might be.

Before long, on one side of the even asphalt highway, a side road appeared leading westward. Covered in gravel, the road apparently had not been used for quite a long time. A companion from Kashi told us that the road led to Mingteke Pass, from where one could enter Afghan territory. However, due to the unstable political conditions in Afghanistan, the Mingteke border station was closed, thus the road was seldom used. He also told

As Marco Polo wrote, one sees nothing here
but the endless barren mountains, not even
birds.

us that not far from the entrance to the road there is a hill on which stands an ancient fortress called Kizikorgan. It is strategically located at a fork in the road that leads to either Afghanistan or Kashmir.

We continued climbing uphill, and soon snow appeared on both sides of the road. As our car approached Kunjirap Pass, everyone in our car began to get slight headaches, effects of the high altitude. At the same time our car slowed down, for there was not enough oxygen at this altitude for the fuel to burn properly.

Our car groaned its way up the pass. At an altitude of 4,800 metres above sea level, this pass is in fact the lowest in the Karakorum Mountains. The effects of crossing mountain passes

top: Small donkey is the most popular means of transportation on the Pamir Highland. The Polos might also ride donkeys to cross this area.

bottom: The pottery sheep unearthed on the Pamir Highland.

over 5,000 metres above sea level would be even more severe, possibly causing vomiting and loss of appetite. Fortunately, once we got over the pass and started descending to a lower altitude, we (and our car) returned to normal.

From the top of the pass we could see snow-capped mountains on all sides. Although the sun was shining brightly overhead, it did not make us feel any warmer. As we were enjoying the view, a mini-bus drove past us and stopped nearby. Two passengers jumped out with their cameras in hand and rushed over to the side of the road. Having only taken a couple of steps, without warning they both slowly dropped to their knees panting heavily, their faces deathly pale. They were helped back to the car after a long rest, and the mini-bus continued on its way. For newcomers to these high mountains doing any kind of exercise, even walking briskly, can be dangerous.

In his book, Marco Polo wrote about the big-horned sheep that today still thrive in the region. Seen here are the cold-enduring yaks.

Today businessmen and tourists from Pakistan have to go through frontier inspection before entering China.

top left: Today crossing the Pamir Highland is almost as difficult as it was in Marco Polo's time.

bottom left: As we descended the Pamir Highland, we passed herdsmen driving their camels with fodder for the winter months.

The Official Start of Our Journey

We were finally at the top of Kunjirap Pass, where we would begin our journey following in the footsteps of Marco Polo. We had been here five years ago, and this time saw no striking changes in the area's appearance, except that there were a few more houses. There were more travellers coming across now than five years ago, which meant that more border officials were needed to man the pass, but everything else seemed little changed.

Over 20 kilometres beyond the pass, we came to the border of China and Pakistan, where a large boundary marker stood. Being 3,900 metres above sea level, the place was very cold even though it was only noon. The barren mountains were treeless, covered only with yellowish grass. Since the Pakistani border army men often come into close contact with the Chinese, they could speak some Mandarin. Though we had only just met, they treated us like old friends. One of them took off his triangular cap and military belt, put them on us and then had a picture taken with us, with the

boundary marker as background. Just then we heard some high-spirited shouting and saw a Pakistani army officer coming towards us with a big bouquet of wild flowers, his face all smiles. What a nice way to start our long, 12,000-kilometre journey!

A Sino-Pakistani boundary marker at Kunjirap Pass, 3,900 metres above sea level.

Kashi – The Largest Bazaar in Xinjiang

喀什
Kashi

塔什库尔干
Taxkorgan

红其拉甫山口
Kunjirap Pass

We shall now leave this country and tell you of the province of Kashgar, which lies towards the east-northeast-east.

Kashgar was once a kingdom, but now it is subject to the Great Khan. It has villages and towns in plenty. The biggest city, and the most splendid, is Kashgar. The inhabitants live by trade and handicraft industry. They have very fine orchards and vineyards and flourishing estates. Cotton grows here in plenty, besides flax and hemp. The soil is fruitful and productive of all the means of life. This country is the starting-point from which many merchants set out to market their wares all over the world... The inhabitants have a language of their own.

– The Travels of Marco Polo

W hile crossing the Hindu Kush Mountains and the Pamir Highland in 1272, frightened and threatened by avalanches, and suffering from severe mountain sickness, the 18-year-old Marco Polo fell seriously ill. A high fever, complicated by terrible dreams during which he talked continuously, took a great toll on his health.

Descending the plateau, he came to the oasis called Kashgar (today's Kashi), which immediately injected him with new life. Once he came down to a height of about 1,000 metres, the mountain sickness that had been torturing him naturally disappeared. Thanks to the warm temperatures, nourishing food and the hospitality of the Uigurs, he soon recovered.

An unusual mosque in Yengisar.

Hundreds of years after Marco Polo's trip, Kashi remains a major city, with people from all over still coming to market their goods, and its residents just as devoted to commerce as they were then.

The small alleys in Kashi in many ways resemble those found in Turkish towns. Courtyards are planted with fruit trees and grape vines, and high-quality cotton is cultivated in the fields. In this

sense, little has changed in the 700 years since
Marco Polo passed through. Here, we had our
own experience of what Marco Polo described as
"a language of their own", a pure Uigur language
which is very hard to understand without an
interpreter.

The day we arrived in Kashi, a Sunday, turned
out to be bazaar day. We had been to many parts of
Xinjiang and visited many bazaars, but the one in
Kashi was by far the largest and most impressive.
We were told that sometimes over 100,000 people

congregate here.

The bazaar only reached its peak after 11:00 in the morning. Once in the bazaar, people lost their individuality and all became part of a huge mass of human beings. One's ears echoed with a continual buzzing sound.

There are small lanes in the bazaar where jackets, skirts, towels and socks in all colours and styles are hung on display, looking like national flags on ocean-going vessels. Uigur women wearing veils peddled square hats that they had embroidered. The most active salesmen were boys of seven or eight who squeezed their way through the crowd, shouting out their wares. From time to time, they would pull in customers, persuading them to buy their goods.

The food stands at the bazaar, however, were

The Uigur Muslims in Kashi have their own particular customs, For example, the veil shown in this picture is rarely seen in northern Xinjiang.

Donkey carts are the most common means of transportation among the Uigurs in Xinjiang.

by far the most popular. On thousands of stoves, a great variety of delicacies were being prepared. The sound of the copper ladles beating against the pots, together with the shouts of the food peddlers, formed a strange symphony, One of the most interesting activities was watching young men making hand-pulled noodles. The dough, which can weigh up to several kilogrammes, must first be rolled and kneaded to become the right texture. Then the cook firmly grips the dough by both ends and swings it up high in the air repeatedly until it is stretched into the shape of a long, thick noodle. He then doubles the dough, swings it, pounds it, rolls it and then repeats the process a dozen times until the dough is of even thickness and as thin as wicker. The finishing touch is the most entertaining part, when the cook twirls the dough in the air in a

Seven hundred years after Marco Polo's arrival in Kashi, it is still a
thriving commercial centre. People from all over the region come to buy,
sell and barter at Kash's huge weekly bazaar.

Every street and lane in Kashi has its own atmosphere, reminiscent of Middle Eastern towns.

top right: These men are making hand-pulled noodles.

bottom right: This boy is a box-maker in the bazaar.

semi-circle and sends the noodles flying right into the boiling pot two metres away.

Other offerings at the bazaar included mutton, which is eaten with one's hands, *nang* or Xinjiang-style baked bread, and kebabs which sizzled appetizingly on the grill. We also happened to see a primitive type of ice-cream maker which was operated by hand. In the dry and hot August weather, ice-cream sales were brisk. We were fortunate to arrive at the most opportune time of the year: the fruit harvesting season, when apples, grapes, watermelon and Hami melon can be

Xinjiang is famous all over the world for its beautiful carpets.

seen everywhere. Melons here were much, much sweeter than those grown in inland provinces, and every time we ate one, our fingers and lips would get sticky. Even our throats seemed to be sticky with sweetness.

The bazaar in Kashi also had a livestock section, which was full of black and white sheep, brown-coloured oxen and gambolling horses and donkeys. For the Uigurs, donkeys are the ideal beast of burden, as they can both carry their owners and pull carts as well. Every Uigur family has its own donkeys. The local donkeys, extremely small compared with the long-legged and tall Guanzhong donkeys in Shaanxi, are flexible, beautiful and very charming. Whenever we saw robust men and grown-up women riding by on their mini donkeys, we felt concerned for the little creatures.

At the livestock market, there was a fascinating etiquette involving the buying and selling of

Sheep have been the companions of Uigur Muslims for generations.

animals. We saw a young Uigur man, a potential customer, grab a donkey, jump on its back and ride off, throwing up clouds of dust. After walking it for a while, the donkey was brought back, having been tested for strength and temperament. If in addition an examination of its teeth proved satisfactory, the deal was sealed. Prospective horse buyers would ride for an even longer distance to test the animal out.

On sale at the bazaar were also various types of foreign goods. Pakistani merchants were regular visitors, and some of them preferred bartering to buying and selling. Though the method was simple, it greatly facilitated the proceedings.

The Pagoda relic in the vicinity of Kashi is the masterpiece of the Buddhist of the ancient Shule Kingdom.(Photo by Zhao Cheng'an)

When bargaining with
these ladies, don t be
fooled by their veils—
they can still see their
customer's every move.

A Muslim chanting the
Koran

HOTAN – AN OASIS IN THE DESERT

We shall pass on to Khotan, which is towards the east-north-east.

Khotan is a province of eight days' journey in extent, which is subject to the Great Khan. The inhabitants all worship Mahomet. It has cities and towns in plenty, of which the most splendid, and the capital of the kingdom, bears the same name as the province, khotan. It is amply stocked with the means of life. Cotton, flax, hemp, and orchards in plenty. The people live by trade and industry; they are not at all war-like.

— The Travels of Marco Polo

In Marco Polo's time, the region of land stretching from Kashi to Hotan (Khotan) was under the control of the Great Khan. People were mainly followers of Islam, as they are today. Then, however, there was also a sizeable community of Nestorian Christians, with their own churches and religious observances.

It took Marco Polo over a week to cover a distance that nowadays only requires a couple of days. Sitting inside our car as we crossed vast expanses of the Taklimakan Desert, we could not help imagining him as he slowly made his way by camel, for centuries the only means of transport for crossing the desert.

Hotan is still a town of affluence, just as Marco Polo described in his book. Arts and crafts are flourishing and a local kind of silk called Aidelis Silk is produced on a household basis. Jade is

The Yengisar Knives.

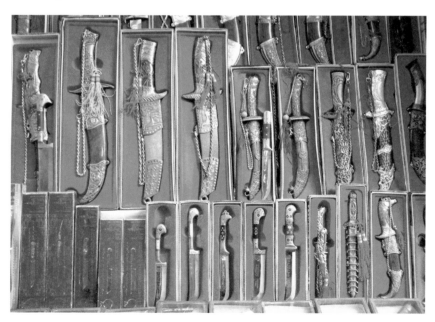

another famous product of the region, as many of the rivers in the area have natural jade in abundant quantities.

Having left Kashi, we crossed several rivers, passed Shule and arrived at Yengisar, which is known throughout China for its superb handmade knives of the same name. At a local market, we saw some knives with plastic handles in all colours, but these were mere imitations of the authentic Yengisar knives, though some of them were exquisitely made. No tourist would come this far to buy a plastic-handled knife, therefore they must be for daily use by the local people. One of the other interesting sights here is the local mosque. The patterns decorating the gate and windows are complex and delicate, exhibiting a high degree of skill and workman-ship.

After covering a long section of the desert, we came upon an oasis crisscrossed with rivers and ditches. As we drove along, we saw fields stretching off into the distance on both sides of the road. This was Shache (Yarkant), a large county in southern Xinjiang. The town has a population of 480,000, over half of which are Han Chinese. In Kashi, people all spoke the Uigur language, but here we needed no interpreter.

Panning for Jade in the Rivers of Hotan

Hotan jade is well-known throughout China for its excellent quality. In the bazaar there were special markets just for selling and buying jade. To attract customers, the jade vendors carried a few stones in

The head of the family always personally inspects the quality of the work.

their hands. Sometimes they tossed the stones up in the air, sometimes they made noise with them. Some clever ones pretended to be looking at their own jade in great admiration so as to attract more customers.

Hotan jade is in fact easy to get in this area. In summer when the snow in the Kunlun Mountains melts, torrents of water rush down the mountain slopes, bringing jade of all sizes to the valleys of Hotan. Having rolled a long distance, they have been chafed smooth and round, and look both pure and beautiful.

Early in the morning, we strolled to a riverbed and saw many jade prospectors already there. One old man was carrying a large piece of black jade and trotting towards the riverside, his face all smiles. Another young man held many small green transparent stones in his hands, which he carefully placed on a piece of white cloth by the sandy riverside. He tried to sell them right away, and there was no shortage of buyers. Not wanting to trouble them to pan for jade personally, potential buyers just stood aside and watched, and when something good was found, they would snap it up at a good price. Then they would take it to the market to resell it at a much higher price.

After dyeing, the thread is spun and is then ready for weaving.

Aidelis Silk – a Local Specialty

Another famous local product in this area is a

special kind of silk called Aidelis Silk. Our next stop, therefore, was to visit a Uigur family which specialized in the weaving of Aidelis Silk. As soon as we entered the house, we were enveloped by the steam rising from a row of cauldrons. Men and women both were hard at work spinning silk by hand, perhaps the most primitive method found in China today. One young girl was spinning the silk on a wooden wheel, while in another room, girls made the silk into thread. Two men then put the thread onto a loom for weaving – a very time-consuming process seldom used these days.

The owner, whose ancestors had also been makers of Aidelis Silk, said, "Hotan's Aidelis Silk is produced on a household basis. Spinning, threading, drawing patterns, dyeing, weaving and so on, it is all done by hand. It takes ten days to complete the making of one bolt of silk fabric. In every household, young and old work together, and in one year, a family like this could produce more than a hundred bolts of silk. My father and

In Hotan every peasant household has a weaving machine. This is a workshop for weaving blanket.

grandfather were both in this line, and they passed it down to us."

When he began working at home, he decided to employ piece-work laborers. In this way two girls could finish a whole day's work in five hours. A bolt of silk fabric could now be woven within two days by two weavers. With the price for one bolt at nine yuan, this was an enormous increase in efficiency over the old methods. In addition, he found that the hired workers worked harder than family members. The women in the family were now responsible just for the making of silk skirts.

In a small Muslim restaurant either the patterns and decorations on the wall or the style of tables and chairs give you a feeling of visiting a common household.

Nowadays, however, it was not as easy as it used to be to market them as young people tend to prefer clothes made of synthetic materials. Machine-made clothes have better patterns and are cheaper, according to them. With these changes in traditional attitudes so prevalent, it is getting harder and harder to sell silk clothes of any kind in this part of the world.

The *turbans* worn by imams are quite unusual. When they are not being worn for Friday prayer services, the imams hang them on a pole outdoors.

Attending a Uigur Wedding

One Saturday our host told us that there was going to be a wedding for two of the local young people. Sure enough, we soon heard the sound of drums and suona trumpets. We said goodbye to our host and hurried out. Following the sound, we found the house where, the wedding was being held. Two hand drums and one suona trumpet were being played and the whole courtyard was full of activity.

Over a large stove, there were two pots full of food. One was pilau rice, which people ate with their hands; the other was cooked meat and vegetables. Every household we visited served their food this way. Like the Han Chinese, the Uigur people throw big parties on the day of a wedding. During the banquet, the groom must play the role of the host and look after his friends and relatives.

At about noon, guests began arriving one by one. Men and women sat on the ground, with men on one side and women on the other. We were first served fried noodles, then rice. On top of the rice,

The architecture of the mosque is decorated with exquisite designs.

there was a layer of mutton. Both the host and the guests used one hand to hold a plate, while the other shoveled the rice into his or her mouth. We thought it rather strange to have a wedding with no wine, as here tea was the only drink. Later we found out that they are not allowed to drink alcohol according to Islamic law.

The tea Uigur people drink has a strange taste, a bit like an herbal broth. We did not like it at first, but wherever we went in southern Xinjiang, we were always entertained with the same tea. Gradually we not only got used to it but even came to love it, eventually thinking that all tea should taste like this. Later we were told that the tea is made of more than ten medicinal herbs and is said to benefit the stomach and intestines. No wonder the four of us had no trouble with our stomachs no matter what we ate or drank. In fact, the Uigur people are very careful about their food, and do not eat anything of a cold nature (antipyretic).

Little boys huddle on the small building of the bride to watch for fun.

These men sitting on the carpet are at a "long banquet" which is the prelude of the wedding ceremony.

For example, they believe that muskmelon has something of a hot nature, and watermelon has a cold nature, so they prefer muskmelons.

At around 6:00 in the evening after the wedding party was over, most of the guests began to leave. Close friends and relatives got on donkey carts and formed a procession of ten to twenty carts to go to the bride's house. As soon as they entered her house, they divided themselves into two groups according to sex. Then they started the wedding feast all over again: mutton, rice and medicinal tea. Having eaten and drunk their fill, the women displayed the dowry and clothes given to the bride. The men, standing around an imam (religious leader), listened to him recite prayers. Then they examined the marriage certificate.

After consulting the bridegroom, four strong young men were chosen to carry the bride out on a carpet. The bride, wearing a new dress and a veil over her head and face, was carried out of the courtyard and put onto a cart. On the way, they

"The mutton rice eaten in hand" is a necessary delicacy in the wedding banquet.

The fascinating small caps on the heads of the three aged women are the exclusive craft of the Uigur women in Yutian area.

were stopped by latecomers, so everyone got out of their carts and began to dance, only later continuing on their way. On that day, several couples got married so all the roads were packed with people and carts. Once the wedding party reached the bride's house, there were more rituals, like "lifting the bride's veil", "joking with the newlyweds" and so on, until midnight.

Nowadays, Uigur brides seldom wear traditional clothes, instead choosing white gauze wedding gowns. Some wear make-up, but they seem unsure of how much to use, sometimes to comical effect. These are signs that the outside world is finally reaching these extremely remote places, albeit slowly and bit by bit. We felt reluctant to leave Hotan. The local customs and the people's colourful lives left a strong impression on us.

Walnuts in Qira and a Mosque in Yutian

The dwellings of Hotan people are all elaborately decorated, very beautiful.

Having left Hotan, we drove east and arrived in Qira. Qira's existence relies on a river, also called Qira. Covering the riverbed were trellises laden with grapes, while walnut trees grew by the riverside. When we arrived, it was walnut season, and people were bringing down the nuts using long poles. Children frolicked about in the water, picking up fallen walnuts and putting them in their baskets.

We set off in the rain for a village outside the town to see how the little Uigur caps were made after we reached Yutian. The caps worn by Uigur women were particularly interesting, all black

The Uigurs living around Yutian are all Muslims, and go to the mosque every Friday to pray.

Those who cannot
enter the mosque
because it is already
full simply pray
outside.

except for the top, which was done in many colours. Looking somewhat like an upside-down black pottery bowl, these caps were different from those we had seen elsewhere and only worn by married women.

In Yutian, there was a mosque built in a unique architectural style. It was Friday and before long, we heard the sound of a man's voice, strong and baritone. We were told that this was the imam, who stood on top of the local mosque to call people to Sunday morning prayer.

When we got out onto the street, we saw people coming out of their houses while tidying up their clothes and caps. A child was being pulled along, one hand holding onto his mother's dress, while the other rubbed

Early in the morning, the imam at the mosque in Yutian stands on the roof to call people to morning prayer.

the sleep out of his eyes. Before long, there was a
big crowd in front of the mosque. Men filed into
the mosque while the women stood outside, since
according to Islamic law they are not allowed
inside the mosque to pray. By the end of the service,
the sun was well up in the sky, cascading golden
sunshine over the top of the mosque, creating a
beautiful sight.

CROSSING THE TAKLIMAKAN DESERT

尼雅大麻扎
Niya mazar

于田
Yutian

民丰
Minfeng

All this province (Charchan) is a tract of sand; and so is the country from Khotan to Pein and from Pein to here. There are many springs of bad and bitter water, though in some places the water is good and sweet. When it happens that an army passes through the country, if it is a hostile one, the people take flight with their wives and children and their beasts two or three days' journey into the sandy wastes to places where they know that there is water and they can live with their beasts.

— The Travels of Marco Polo

Pein and Charchan mentioned by Marco Polo were the names of two ancient areas that flourished in his time. The ruins of the city of Pein lie in a place called Laodamagou in the Taklimakan, and Charchan Province was probably the region between Yutian and Ruoqiang.

This section of our journey would take us from Yutian to Minfeng, not a great distance on the map, but it turned out to be one of the most arduous parts of our trip. Travelling across vast expanses of the Taklimakan Desert by jeep, we began to understand why camels are still the most reliable means of transport.

Like Marco Polo, we also found precious little in the way of spring water, needing to carry all potable water with us wherever we went. Thankfully, hostile armies no longer maraud their way through the desert – for us the greatest enemies were mosquitoes and the endless, all-consuming sand.

Unlike going to the bazaar, going on a pilgrimage to the mazar is a sacred, solemn activity for devout Muslims. Muslims in the rest of the world make pilgrimages to Mecca, but Xinjiang Muslims go on pilgrimage to the mazar in Minfeng, where it is said that a legendary Islamic prophet is buried. Each August, the Uigurs in southern Xinjiang, and even followers of Islam in northern Xinjiang, drive their ox carts, mule carts and tractors through deserts and over snow-covered mountains to Minfeng.

Of course we did not want to miss this rare opportunity.

A Difficult Pilgrimage

We drove along the banks of the Niya River towards the vast desert, first on a sand road, then on a dirt track and eventually just through the sand. Our jeep went slower and slower the further we penetrated the desert, and sank into one pit of sand after another.

The Uigurs' tractors were ten times better than our little jeep for travelling in the desert. With large trailers carrying people of all ages plus several calves and lambs, they chugged along ahead of us, leaving behind a trail of black smoke.

Before we knew it, night was upon us. We had started out at 5:00 p.m. and it was now nearly 10:00; we had spent more than four hours on the sand "road". When we calculated the distance, we found that we had only covered 50 kilometres! To reach the Niya mazar, we had more than 40 kilometres to go, but when we learned that the road ahead was

This lone pilgrim prays in the direction of the mazar.

easier, we began to relax.

The temperature dropped quickly after the sun had set and the unbearable heat of the day passed. Our drinking water was nearly gone so we would have to drink sparingly to make it last until we arrived at our destination. We bumped violently along the rough sand road, which was illuminated only by the jeeps dazzling headlights. The dust was so suffocating we could scarcely breathe. Luckily we had brought wet towels with us when we left, which now came in very useful as a cover for our mouths. Breathing was difficult, but at least it prevented the disgusting dust from getting into our mouths.

We reached a village called Kabakasgan at

The imams in Minfeng pray to Allah.

midnight. From the village to the Niya mazar it was only five kilometres. Weary though we were, we resisted the temptations of comfortable lodgings and delicious food and continued on our way, determined to stay near the mazar so as to catch the religious service that would take place there the next morning.

After another half hour of difficult driving, at 1:00 a.m. we reached Tulkiqikol, a small village of just 15 households which serves as a lodging place for pilgrims. In the light of our jeep's headlights, we saw pilgrims from all parts of Xinjiang sleeping

An imam tells us the story of this man, who died during an Islamic Jihad about 800 years ago.

top: The ancient city of Taxkorgan is also called Stone City, it is said to have a history of over one thousand years.

bottom: The relic of Niya ancient city. (Photo by Liu Yusheng)

on the ground in the open spaces between the cottages. The chugging of our jeep's engine and its headlights awakened not only the sound sleepers who had travelled all day through the desert, but also the imams living in the village. They all came out to welcome us and wish us a pleasant journey.

We felt elated; after having travelled for more than eight gruelling hours, we had finally arrived at Xinjiang's Mecca. Our hosts quickly treated us to tea, *nang* cakes and soft, sweet melons. No midnight snack in the world could have been better

than this one. As we enjoyed our food and drank the tea, we listened to the imam as he related to us the history of the Niya mazar.

A "holy meal" is eaten after the mazar has concluded.

A Bedtime Story

In fluent Mandarin, the imam told us that an Islamic prophet, a fifth generation descendant of Mohammed, was buried in the Niya mazar. In the middle of the Tang Dynasty, he led his troops on an eastern expedition during an Islamic Jihad (holy war). His army went straight into China, took Kashi and then reached Hotan, where he met a strong opponent, the Tubo Regime, a hegemonious power in the Western Regions. During the fierce battle that ensued, he was defeated and killed on a sand dune. His body was buried on the spot – the present-day Niya mazar.

In the depths of the desert, about ten kilometres north of the village, are the ruins of the original

The local inhabitants welcome pilgrims coming from afar.

town of Niya, which many modern scholars believe was the capital of the Jingjue Kingdom as recorded in *the History of the Han Dynasty*. The site of the ruins stretches 22 kilometres from south to north and six kilometres from east to west. Among the ruins are the remains of temples, living quarters, gardens and bridges.

In the depths of the night, the unbearable heat of the day gradually retreated, and a gentle breeze began to blow. Somehow we felt more comfortable lying on the sand in the middle of the Taklimakan Desert, with a few mud houses and tall trees nearby. Everywhere on the uneven sand, beside the tractors and under the eaves, the Islamic faithful slept, looking like an army camp in ancient times.

Morning Prayer in the Desert

At 7:30 a.m. (Beijing time, but only 5:30 in Xinjiang), the day had not yet broken, but the

pilgrims sleeping all around the village had already got up and were beginning to walk to the mosque. We got up as well, and followed them with our flashlights.

At 9:00 when the sun had completely risen, people flocked out of the mosque towards the vast desert. They walked in separate groups divided into men and women. We followed them through a small mazar and arrived at a high sand hill. From the top of the hill we saw an earthen house in the distance, around which were flagpoles with small banners hung on them. This was the big mazar.

As they approached it, the Muslims began to go down on their knees to pray, repeating the process every few steps. On the hill behind the mazar was a large shed, where crowds of people knelt on the ground reading the Koran. Outside the mazar were also crowds of people kneeling on the ground reciting scriptures, while waiting for their turn to enter to do worship. No one spoke, and all wore a

This is the Niya mazar, considered by Uigur Muslims to be the Mecca of Xinjiang.

top right: This framework is the entrance to the Niya mazar.

bottom right: Under the morning sunshine, the Muslims faithfully recite the Koran.

serious, solemn look on their faces.

In the distant forest below the mazar, a large group of women knelt on the ground around a bonfire, weeping bitterly. Beside them were crowds of men who had abandoned their usual behaviour and were also weeping in loud and booming voices. Wondering if someone had died recently, we asked someone and were told that they were pouring out the grievances and suffering concealed in their hearts to their prophet, in the hope of obtaining consolation and enlightenment to relieve them from their pain.

Around the mazar were poles with colourful banners, and around the entrance dry sheepskins were hung and stuffed with straw, offerings presented by worshippers. With great respect, the pilgrims took off their shoes and entered quietly. The imam pointed out to us a coffin lying on an earthen platform covered by cloth. Inside the coffin was the body of Mohammed's fifth descendant, who had spread the word of

top: Since Muslim women are not allowed to enter the mosque, they form groups outside to pray.

bottom: The broken pottery pot piece unearthed in Xinjiang. The patterns on which show apparent Western art style.

Females are not allowed to enter the mosque. This woman is praying piously outside the mosque.

Islam to this area.

Xinjiang's Own Mecca

Fortunately, making pilgrimages to the mazar in Minfeng County did not cost that much. In fact, seven trips to Minfeng was equivalent to one trip to Mecca. It was not too difficult for ordinary people to visit the Niya mazar seven separate times in their lifetime. This was why the Uigurs in Kuqa, Shache, Hotan and even in Kashi and Koria would travel on buses, tractors and mule carts for several days and nights to pay homage.

It is said that there are a number of mazars in the Hotan region, each visited in different seasons. Buried in all these mazar are Muslim heroes, but the most famous and prestigious of all is the Niya mazar, with the annual pilgrimage held in August and September. Before or after this time no pilgrims come here – and once we arrived, we understood the reason. In spring, strong sand storms arise which continue for more than ten days at a time. You are not even able to stand up, let alone walk. In autumn and winter it is too cold, accommodations too few, and camping in the open is absolutely impossible. August and September, therefore, are the best times to make pilgrimages.

Buried Cities and Shifting Sands — Onward to Dunhuang

民丰 Minfeng　　且末 Qiemo　　若羌 Ruoqiang　　米兰 Miran　　茫崖 Mangnai　　敦煌 Dunhuang
阿尔金山口 Altun Mountain Pass　　老茫崖 Old Mangnai　　冷湖 Lenghu

At the point where the traveller enters the Great Desert, is a big city called Lop.... I can tell you that travellers who intend to cross the desert rest in this town for a week to refresh themselves and their beasts. At the end of the week they stock up with a month's provisions for themselves and their beasts. Then they leave the town and enter the desert.

This desert is reported to be so long that it would take a year to go from end to end; and at the narrowest point it takes a month to cross it. It consists entirely of mountains and sand and valleys....

When a man is riding by night through this desert and something happens to make him loiter and lose touch with his companions, by dropping asleep or for some other reason, and afterwards he wants to rejoin them, then he hears spirits talking in such a way that they seem to be his companions. Sometimes, indeed, they even hail him by name. Often these voices make him stray from the path, so that he never finds it again. And in this way many travellers have been lost and have perished.

— The Travels of Marco Polo

The next leg of our journey is a long one, from Minfeng all the way across the desert to Dunhuang. Unfortunately, we were only able to follow in Marco Polo's footsteps as far as Ruoqiang, near to the ancient city of Lop (also known as Loulan, near Lop Nur), which is now buried deep beneath the sand.

Seven centuries ago, Marco Polo and many other travellers stopped over in Lop to stock up on supplies for the long and perilous journey through desert to Hami. Although it did not take him a year to get through the desert, he did spend at least

The tall diversiform-leaved poplar tree is the hallmark of a desert oasis. It is able to grow and even flourish, with deep roots and luxuriand leaves, as long as there is a little water in the sand.

a month reaching Hami before continuing on to Dunhuang.

Nowadays it might not take that long, but in any case no one ventures any more into that vast, inhospitable desert wasteland. The desert has encroached upon and engulfed more and more territory as time has gone by, making it virtually a no man's land. Both today and in Marco Polo's time, as he wrote, "one must go for a day and a night without finding water" and "there is nothing to eat at all". This, combined with his eerie tales of voices and apparitions, made us very happy indeed that there is now a state road that leads to Dunhuang, where we would be back in "civilization".

From Minfeng we continued our way eastward for 300 kilometres and arrived in Qiemo. Along the way the scenery was unexpectedly beautiful. Tall diversiform-leaved poplars and low reed clumps lined the road. Beyond, the land was covered with lush green grass on which cattle and sheep grazed leisurely. The Kunlun Mountains receded into the background until they finally disappeared.

We stopped only for a short rest at Qiemo, and

This is a type of large-wheeled vehicle which one can use to cross the desert (if one dares), thus avoiding the 1,000-kilometre detour our authors had to make.

From the Altun
Mountains one can see
the Qiangtang Plateau on
the horizon, home of the
Altun Nature Reserve

then resumed our journey. We had to drive another 371 kilometres before we reached Ruoqiang. Once out of Qiemo, the greenery was quickly replaced by yellow sand which stretched far into the distance. One long section of road ahead was completely covered by sand. Surrounding it were endless stretches of shifting sand dunes, moved about by the wind all year round.

When we arrived at Ruoqiang it was already midnight. After travelling 680 kilometres in one day we were totally exhausted and went to bed as soon as we checked into a guesthouse. When we woke up it was already past 10:00 in the morning. It was a sunny day, and outside the summer heat was suffocating.

According to the Chinese classic tale *Journey to the West*, Tripitaka crossed this river on his way to India in search of Buddhist scriptures.

Ruoqiang is a small county seat with streets – not very long, but neat and tidy and few passers-by.

The Ruins of the Ancient City of Miran

At daybreak the following day we continued on our journey. After driving eastward for 70 kilometres we came to Miran, the oldest land reclamation area in Xinjiang. Around 2,000 years ago during the Western Han Dynasty (206 B.C.-A.D. 24), it was an army reclamation area called Yixun, belonging to the domain of the State of Loulan, one of the 36 states in the Western Regions. The ancient city of Loulan, or Lop, lies buried deep in the desert.

These mounds of rubble are all that remains of the ancient city of Miran.

Sometimes, stones of bizarre shape under the effect of aeolian erosion can be found in desert.

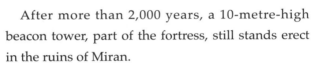

After more than 2,000 years, a 10-metre-high beacon tower, part of the fortress, still stands erect in the ruins of Miran.

From the fortress we could see a temple which was surrounded by groups of tombs. Standing out among them was a cone-shaped mausoleum, around which were the remains of civilian residences. This was a strong reminder that this was once a densely-populated, prosperous city, with fields and irrigation channels. In the past, all travellers from Ruoqiang to Lop had to come through Miran. After this, the next city one comes to is Dunhuang, at the westernmost end of the Hexi Corridor.

During his visit to China 700 years ago, Marco Polo travelled this same route. He stayed for a period at the city of Lop for a rest and to prepare provisions for his forthcoming desert journey. He wrote in his book that a stock of provisions should be laid in for a month before crossing the desert. At

top left: At the end of the 19ᵗʰ century, foreign expeditionist came to Lop Nur.

top middle: The authors' long, arduous journey through southern Xinjiang is nearing its end, as Qinghai Province looms in the distance.

top right: The ancient inhabitants' articles for daily use unearthed from the ancient tombs of Loulan

bottom: The tomb relic of ancient Loulan. (photo by Li Xueliang)

that time this desert was considered to be the abode of many evil spirits, which distracted travellers to their destruction with most extraordinary illusions. For hundreds of years, an unknown number of soldiers, merchants, monks, travellers and exiles met their death on this perilous road.

A World of Asbestos

Returning back to Ruoqiang from Miran, we

In Ruoqiang, the local people make a kind of flat bread as big as that made by the Han Chinese in the Hexi Corridor.

headed eastward and before long the Altun Mountains came into view. Greyish yellow rocks covered the mountains and gravel danced in the air. It was summertime in other areas, a season of thriving vegetation, but although we searched high and low, we could find nothing green.

Setting off at 10:00 a.m., by 3:00 we had come to an asbestos mining area, actually the town of Mangnai on the border between Xinjiang and

This 104-year-old man was a native of the Lop Nur area. When he was 35, his family was forced to move to the Miran area due to a severe drought that dried up all the lakes.

Qinghai. It is an open-air asbestos mine operated by both machine and manpower. Carried by strong winds, the white asbestos powder permeates the air over an area of dozens of kilometres. It settles on human bodies, roof tops, electric wires and posts, a veritable world of asbestos.

The local people cannot escape from asbestos, especially since it constitutes the main source of their income. They can only wear face masks to protect themselves, creating quite a strange sight.

Marco Polo also wrote about asbestos in his book, calling it "salamander". He mentioned that how asbestos were mined, processed and weaved into cloth in his book.

In their leisure time people gather together and listen to the imam discuss the Koran.

And he said that one of these cloths is now at Rome; it was sent to the Pope by the Great Khan as a valuable gift, and for this reason the sacred napkin of our lord Jesus Christ was wrapped in it."

In fact, when Marco Polo first returned to his native Venice and mentioned the existence of such a material, his country people all laughed at him, thinking he had imagined it.

An Oil City in the Desert

After leaving Mangnai we headed southeastward, temporarily bidding farewell to the bald Altun Mountains and entering the desert area of the Qaidam Basin. Having passed through Youshashan, we came to the banks of Gashu Lake, a salt lake. Its deep blue water makes a striking contrast to the yellow sandy shores, which are themselves covered with a thick layer of salt and alkaline as white as snow.

Driving eastward we stopped at another town also called Mangnai, but this one only consists of a few houses built of mud and most of them are inns accommodating drivers. The whole place is like a solitary hidden rock standing in the vast ocean of the desert. From here we turned northward and the topography began to change. The ground here was covered with strangely-shaped rocks overgrown with white powdered crystals which we were told were Glauber's salt (sodium sulphate).

At Niubiziliang we returned to the embrace of the Altun Mountains, then turning eastward we soon reached Lenghu, an oil city in Qinghai

Province.

The city of Lenghu was originally a salt lake. Located at a high altitude and in a frigid zone, it has no vegetation. The discovery of oil, however,

top: An old caretaker at the Jungar Temple followed us closely for fear that we might touch the sacrificial objects.

bottom: Although quite remote, this place is not totally cut off from the outside world, as seen by these posters of Chinese and foreign films.

has brought both people and vitality to this barren area. Today there are shopping arcades, cinemas, a TV station and hotels, but still one sees neither animals nor plants anywhere.

Departing from Lenghu our car climbed up Dangjin Pass, the main passage leading to Gansu Province. A line consisting of all kinds of vehicles ran up the spiralling mountain road. Our car crawled up laboriously, and after passing through Dangjin Pass we turned northward and descended

A Glauber's salt (sodium sulphate) mine in the Qaidam Basin.

down the steep road, Mt. Dangjin is 4,000 metres above sea level, while Dunhuang is only 1,000 metres above sea level, therefore we made a drop of nearly 3,000 metres in just 100 kilometres. Our car glided down swiftly to Dunhuang, consuming no more than two litres of petrol.

In the Lop desert which Marco Polo had traversed.

A TEN-DAY TRIP ACROSS THE HEXI CORRIDOR

敦煌
Dunhuang

安西
Anxi

嘉峪关
Jiayuguan

酒泉
Jiuquan

张掖
Zhangye

武威
Wuwei

山丹马场
Shandan Military
Steed Ranch

兰州
Lanzhou

When the traveller has ridden for these thirty days of which I have spoken across the desert, he reaches a city called Sa-chau, lying towards the east-north-east, which is subject to the Great Khan. It lies in a province called Tangut, whose inhabitants are all idolaters.... They do not live by trade, but on the profit of the grain which they harvest from the soil. They have many abbeys and monasteries, all full of idols of various forms to which they make sacrifices and do great honour and reverence.

Let us now pass on to Kan-chau, a large and splendid city in Tangut proper and the capital of the whole province....

When the traveller leaves Kan-chau, he journeys eastward for five days through a country haunted by spirits, whom he often hears talking in the night, till he reaches a kingdom called Erginul This is subject to the Great Khan...

...There are many wild cattle here, as big as elephants and very handsome in appearance...

This country produces the best and finest musk in the world.

– The Travels of Marco Polo

Although the names of the places Marco Polo mentions have naturally changed in 700 years, most of them are still in the same locations. For example Sa-chau is today's well-known city of Dunhuang, whose grottoes and Buddhist statues were extant long before Marco Polo's arrival. The province he refers to as Tangut was a large province of the Tartars (Mongols) ruled by the Great Khan, roughly covering today's Gansu and Shaanxi provinces and Ningxia Hui Autonomous Region. Kan-chau is today's Zhangye, and the kingdom called Erginul is the area around Wuwei, both in Gansu Province.

Throughout his book Marco Polo continually labeled the local people "idolaters", because they worshipped idols and images that he neither recognized nor understood. We know now that what he saw was most likely Buddhism, as there is a great deal of very ancient Buddhist art in this region. It is even quite possible that he visited the Big Buddha Temple in Zhangye, today a well-known tourist site, as his description of a temple he visited there matches it perfectly: "These huge idols are recumbent, and groups of lesser ones are set round about them...."

In fact, much of what Marco Polo saw is still the same today. The "wild cattle" (yaks) still roam the hills (although they are not quite as big as elephants!) and musk deer still live in the region. Few people believe these days that there are spirits that haunt the Hexi (Gansu) Corridor, but a great many of the customs and ways of life that he observed are practiced not only here but in other

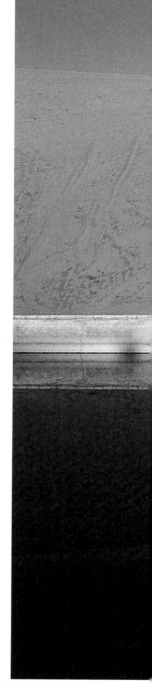

This man-made
reservoir feeds the
Crescent Moon
Spring at Singing
Sand Hill.

parts of China as well. Travelling in these parts, one gets a strong feeling for the history and continuity of this ancient civilization.

In ancient times the Hexi (West of the Yellow River) Corridor was accessible by two alternative routes from Central Asia, either through Yangguan Pass in the south or through Yumenguan Pass in the north, both leading to the ancient city of Dunhuang. Marco Polo and his party reached Dunhuang, then called Sa-chau, by way of Lop Nur and Yangguan Pass. The vast waters in Lop Nur, the bustling, ancient town of Lop and the solid walls of Yangguan Pass have all been swept away by history, but Dunhuang still enjoys prosperity.

Twelve years ago, one of our authors stayed for a time in Dunhuang. Then, everywhere there was

The value of the sculptures and murals in the Mogao Grottoes increases yearly. Marco Polo often mentioned seeing temples and the worship of "idols" in his book.

yellow clay; even the houses were built of clay. There was only one main street and even a small hotel was difficult to find. Now, Dunhuang has become a city, crisscrossed by wide, clean streets with buses going to all points.

Among the crowds quite a few Westerners and Japanese Buddhists can be seen, the latter of which take a special interest in the Buddhist tradition here. The influx of foreign tourists has made the hotel industry a booming business, with over a dozen major hotels to choose from. Even so, they are all packed out during peak seasons, leaving hardly any room for those who come too late.

We visited the Mingsha (Singing Sand) Hill to see if there had been any changes after twelve years. Indeed there were, for it seemed as if the hill had actually moved from its original position. We slowly climbed up the hill, the grains of sand warm under our feet and the breeze carrying a welcome coolness. Standing on the hilltop at twilight, the sand dunes below were studded with the moving shadows of Chinese and foreign tourists. As the curious tourists slid down the slopes of the sand dunes, sand rolled down to the accompaniment of shouts and laughter.

The multicolour sculpture of the Mogao Grottoes.

Perhaps this is how the Singing Sand Hill had managed to change its location.

On the distant tracks leading into the hill, camels scurried about, ready to be hired by tourists for rides to and from the sand dunes. After sliding down the hill, we found ourselves by the side of the Yueya (Crescent Moon) Spring. The water in the spring reflected the violet sky and pinkish-white clouds, while reeds nearby stirred in the gentle breeze. It was already 9:30 p.m., but the sun had not yet set. The slanting sun rays penetrated between the dunes and enveloped the hill in a golden glow.

Zhang Qian had ever reached Loulan when he visited the Western Regions as an envoy.

Dunhuang – a Gathering Place for Old and New Immigrants

We came back to Dunhuang at 10:30 p.m., when night finally fell. Sitting at a small restaurant by the roadside, we heard people around us talking in the

northern Chinese dialect.

The manager of our hotel, on the other hand, spoke with a Central Plains accent, which was soon confirmed when she told us that she was a native of Henan Province. Thirty years before, almost half of the people in her village were driven out by famine, forced to travel along the ancient Silk Road to eke out a living in the Hexi Corridor.

In time, the relatively fertile regions such as Dunhuang, Anxi, Jiuquan and Zhangye became a second homeland for people from the eastern provinces. In fact, the so-called "natives of Hexi" may be traced, for the most part, to descendants of immigrants from eastern provinces or soldiers sent to guard the frontiers throughout history. The real natives were either forced to move to Central Asia due to endless wars between ethnic groups, or they have been assimilated through peaceful coexistence with the Han people.

Today, as in Marco Polo's time, the people in Dunhuang are still basically engaged in agriculture. This area is well-known for its peaches, apricots, pears and cotton, as well as its wheat. Located at the lowest end of the Hexi Corridor and blessed with a warm climate, plenty of sunshine and abundant water resources, Dunhuang has been able to preserve at least some of its historical importance over the centuries.

However, the remark made by Marco Polo that the people here "do not live by trade" no longer holds true. Now, almost all farmers in the vicinity of the city do some business in addition to their farming. Other than selling fruit, cereals or cotton,

they might also open restaurants, inns or organize transportation teams. Some even bring their camels or horses to the Singing Sand Hill and solicit tourists to take rides around the sand dunes.

Early the next day, we paid a visit to the Mogao Grottoes. In the caves, the small courtyard in which she had spent two months was still there, looking much as it did back then. There was the small cabin she had used as a darkroom, but the young tree outside the window had grown quite big. Nevertheless, the caves are now under much stricter management rules. Twelve years before, she had freely entered the nearly one hundred caves to take photographs, but this time was not so easy. After showing our identification documents and doing much pleading, we were finally permitted to climb up the hilltop to take a bird's-eye photograph of the Mogao Grottoes.

A Melon Festival in Anxi

Soon after midday, the air became dry and hot. Our car left Dunhuang and pulled onto Highway 313 for Anxi. Blasts of hot wind rushed into the car and against our faces. Before us, the smooth black asphalt road, melting and shining under the scorching sun, stretched far into the distance. There were hardly any pedestrians or approaching vehicles anywhere.

As we drove into Anxi, fields, trees, villages and people appeared suddenly along the roads. We happened to arrive just as the Melon Festival of the Hexi Corridor was being held. We drove directly

to the melon market to quench the thirst caused by our tiring journey, as well as to see this rare event. It was just towards the end of melon season, and both muskmelons and brilliant Yellow River honey melons were piled high everywhere.

Adults were busy selling the melons, while children slept lazily on melon piles. People were crowding around the vendors and haggling in loud voices. After being weighed and paid for, the melons were loaded onto trucks and tractors. Bustling Anxi County still lives up to its ancient name of "the Melon Prefecture". Having eaten all we could, we filled up our car with the delicious fruit. Heat and fatigue had vanished, and we were on the road again, refreshed and in high spirits.

The highway from Dunhuang to Anxi runs parallel to the ancient Silk Road. Along the way one can see beacon towers built during the Han and Tang dynasties.

The Hexi Corridor is a peculiar gift of nature. It stretches over 1,200 kilometres from east to west, but its width from north to south varies from a mere 10 kilometres to 100 kilometres at most. To

The caravan marching in desert.

its north is an expanse of barren deserts, and to its south rise the lofty Qilian Mountains, covered with snow. The Qilian Mountains run parallel to the Hexi Corridor for over 1,000 kilometres, providing irrigation through the melted snow and ice that flow down the mountains. For this reason, this is the most fertile area in Gansu Province, with abundant harvests and rich grasslands for raising animals.

A Night in Jiayuguan

On our third day in the Hexi Corridor it began raining, a rare experience in this region. It was a very fine drizzle, just enough to moisten the air but not enough to alter our plans. We had arranged that day to pay a visit to the ancient Wei and Jin tombs and Caohu. Our guide led us into the bleak desert, where tombs from both the Wei and Jin dynasties (220-420) were discovered in 1972. One of the most important discoveries were bricks with pictures painted on them, a surprise to both Chinese and foreign archaeologists. The bricks were either inscribed or painted with scenes from

the dead person's life, as well as scenes depicting daily activities of the society at that time, such as farming, picking mulberry leaves, raising silkworms or feeding cattle.

If these painted bricks were realistic works by ancient artists, it may be inferred that this place was a bustling communications hub about 2,000 years ago. According to the staff at the Administration Office of Cultural Relics, if all the tombs in this region were excavated and connected into an "underground palace", they would cover almost as much space as the terra-cotta army of the Qin Dynasty found near Xi'an.

The Jiayuguan Fortress at the westernmost end of the Great Wall.

Our next stop, Caohu, adjoins a stretch of desert and people make a living by raising camels and sheep. The continuous rain brought joy to the local people, who regarded it as a rare blessing by nature; but to us, the rain meant it was impossible to photograph.

August is the wheat harvesting season in the Hexi Corridor. Watermelons are now also in season, providing a welcome refreshment for the hard-walking farmers.

Towards evening, the rain stopped. The sky appeared an extraordinary blue, and the white walls of the houses were tinged pink by the red clouds. We rushed to Jiayuguan Fortress and took snapshots of the magnificent colours. In the distance, the Qilian Mountains were hidden behind a white veil – snow on the mountain tops and rain at the foot of the mountains. The western sky was a surging sea of red clouds, which heralded fine weather for the next day.

Wanting to get some photos of the fortress at sunrise, at 7:00 in the morning we drove our car again towards Jiayuguan Fortress. Unfortunately, our car got stuck again and we had no choice but

to walk the rest of the way. Standing against the snow-capped Qilian Mountains, Jiayuguan Fortress radiated a red light, like a palace inhabited by supernatural beings. At the foot of the fortress, we met a guide for a group of German tourists, who corroborated yesterday's weather prediction, saying that he had been here several times but had never seen such fine weather.

On to Zhangye

On our fifth day, we came to Jiuquan (meaning "wine spring"). The fatigue that had accumulated over the past few days and the disturbance to our regular habits had tired us down and given us indigestion. We had to brace ourselves up to see the newly renovated "Wine Spring" and to have a cursory glance of the city, and then spent the rest of the day lying in the Jiuquan Hotel.

The relic of ancient Yangguan Fortress. Many major towns on the ancient Silk Road disappeared, only the remnants of the city walls being left.

Still feeling giddy, we continued on our way and

reached Zhangye on the sixth day. We visited the Big Buddha Temple, a wooden pagoda and saw sections of the Ming Dynasty (1368-1644) Great Wall ruins.

Marco Polo arrived in Zhangye around 1272 and stayed there for approximately one year. In his book, he gave detailed description of Zhangye, referring to it as Kan-chau and calling it "a large and splendid city".

On the seventh day, we set out from Zhangye early in the morning and made our way southward to visit the Shandan Military Steed Ranch. We turned southeast at Nangucheng along the Qilian

Mountains and finally reached Damaying Prairie, along the Shandan River. For centuries, this prairie has been a luxuriant natural pastureland. It is said that since the Han Dynasty, and through many other dynasties, it was used as a horse ranch. During the Sui and Tang dynasties (581-907) there were over 100,000 horses here. The Northern Wei, Western Xia and Yuan Dynasties also designated this place as an imperial horse ranch.

The Shandan Military Steed Ranch was once an imperial horse breeding centre.

Nourished by the water and grasses of Shandan, the Shandan horse is virile, elegant and strong-willed, a favourite of both the military and farmers. At present, the Shandan Military Steed Ranch covers an area of over 200,000 hectares, the largest of its kind in Asia. In addition to the grassland and snow-capped Qilian Mountains, there is a large reservoir and a vast stretch of primitive forest in Shandan, making it a most intriguing place.

The military steed ranch has many sub-ranches. As we drove aimlessly across mountains and grassland, we found ourselves in the domain of the No.1 sub-ranch. People working in the ranch are mainly engaged in raising horses and farming, including growing highland barley and rape. This year, a serious drought had hit the grassland. It was just early autumn, but the grass had already begun to wither and turn yellow. However, we were told that it only takes one good rainfall to make the grass green again.

Marco Polo's "Wild Cattle"

In the evening, we left the ranch and continued

Changcheng (the Great Wall)
Village in Wuwei lies close to
the western-most edge of the
Tengger Desert. It is possible
that Marco Polo entered
the desert from here, going
eastward to Ningxia.

on our way along the northern slope of the Qilian Mountains until we reached Yongchang, where we stayed the night. On our eighth day we left Yongchang and again penetrated the bleak desert. At noon, we arrived in Wuwei.

Wuwei is located at the easternmost end of the Hexi Corridor. It is shielded by mountains on three sides, and to its northeast lies the great Tengger Desert. With fertile land and ample sunshine, coupled with the advantage of being irrigated by melted snow from the Qilian Mountains, it is known as "Silver Wuwei", meaning a land of abundance.

The history of the ancient city of Wuwei can be traced back over 2,000 years. It was under the occupation of the Xiongnu (Huns) in the early Western Han Dynasty. Later, in order to open up a passageway to Central Asia, Emperor Wudi (r. 140-87 B.C.) sent two generals to defeat the Xiongnu troops and establish Wuwei Prefecture.

This state-owned shopping centre in Wuwei was once the site of a brothel on the Silk Road.

Towards the end of the Western Han Dynasty it began to be called Liangzhou, meaning "the cool prefecture", presumably because morning time is rather cold in this region. In Marco Polo's time it was called Erginul, and then later became today's Wuwei.

Marco Polo offered a detailed description of Wuwei in his book. He said that cereals were plentiful, and the inhabitants were all Buddhists ("idolaters"). He also wrote that he had seen a kind of large animal, "covered with long hair, except on the back, and ... white and black in colour. The length of their hair is fully three palms. They are so handsome that they are a wonder to behold." He wrote that it was a hardy species and, after being tamed, could be used as a beast of burden.

This animal can only be the yak, raised by the Tibetan people in the Qilian Mountains at that time. Later, as we were crossing over Wushaoling Pass in our car, we spotted groups of long-haired yaks on the grassy slopes. Today, as in Marco Polo's time, they are used for ploughing, as beasts of burden, or for riding.

A Funeral and a "Red Light District"

On the ninth day, as we roamed about Wuwei, we came upon a funeral procession. The coffin was sheltered by a canopy of blue cotton curtains and decorated magnificently with white couplets, colourful wreaths and objects made of paper. Anything the dead might yearn for but could not get in this life, is made for him – albeit of paper –

after his death. This age-old Chinese tradition goes back centuries, and was observed by Marco Polo during his travels to this area.

What he saw was actually a "marriage" of two dead children, whose parents arranged for the two to be together in the afterlife, also a custom still practiced today in certain regions. He described the funeral-marriage in great detail, writing, "They draw pictures on paper of men in the guise of slaves, and of horses, clothes, coins, and furniture, and then burn them; and they declare that all these become the possessions of their children in the next world...."

According to Chinese tradition, the dead must lie in state for seven days for relatives and friends to pay their last respects. Here, however, this occurs while a tape recorder blasts out local operas or Western music, or a folk orchestra plays old music pieces from the Northwest to the accompaniment of a suona, a woodwind instrument. But with the exception of the tape recorder and Western music, the customs practiced here are almost exactly the same as they were 700 years ago.

On the tenth day, not long after we left Wuwei and made our way southeastward, we began our ascent of the Wushaoling Mountains. After we passed Gulang, the mountains became increasingly steep. The flat and unobstructed Hexi Corridor was reaching its end. With a great deal of effort, our car crossed over the Wushaoling Pass, passed Tianzhu and Yongdeng, and headed towards Lanzhou, one of the most important cities in Northwest China.

TRAVERSING THE ANCIENT
LAND OF THE WESTERN XIA

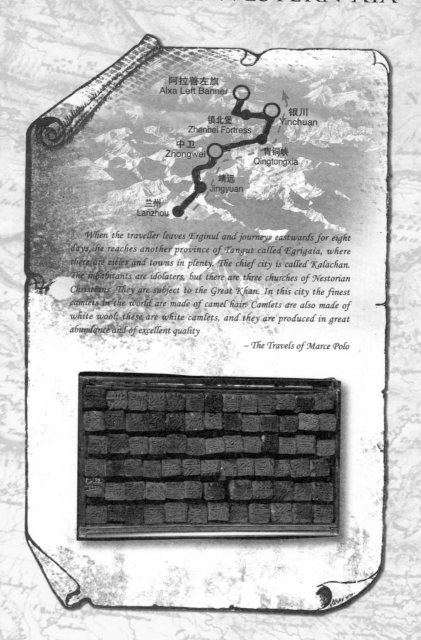

When the traveller leaves Erginul and journeys eastwards for eight days, he reaches another province of Tangut called Egrigaia, where there are cities and towns in plenty. The chief city is called Kalachan. The inhabitants are idolaters, but there are three churches of Nestorian Christians. They are subject to the Great Khan. In this city the finest camlets in the world are made of camel hair. Camlets are also made of white wool: these are white camlets, and they are produced in great abundance and of excellent quality

— *The Travels of Marco Polo*

T oday the area referred to by Marco Polo as Egrigaia is Ningxia Hui Autonomous Region, although there have been changes with respect to its size and boundaries. The city of Kalachan was probably the capital of ancient Western Xia Kingdom, and the "camlets" mentioned in his book are apparently a kind of cloth made of camel wool. We, however, saw no camels until we were approaching Inner Mongolia, where customs are more similar than in Ningxia to those he observed over 700 years ago.

This part of our journey took us from Lanzhou north to the Helan Mountains, following the Yellow River. We had actually made a detour by coming to Lanzhou, not on Marco Polo's route. His contingent, escorted by the imperial guards of the Yuan Dynasty (1271-1368), took a short cut along the southern fringes of the Tengger Desert, spending no more than eight days travelling from Wuwei to Yinchuan in Ningxia, a distance of over 500 kilometres.

The Yellow River bathed in the brilliance of the rising sun.

In Lanzhou we rested for some time to refresh ourselves and to overhaul the vehicle that had carried us for over 4,000 kilometres. We set out early on a September morning, leaving Lanzhou and driving northwards to the town of Zhongwei, where we would pick up the route followed by Marco Polo.

We had lunch at Jingyuan, and while chatting with the restaurant owner, we saw out of the window a drum tower in the town centre. He told us that almost every town in Gansu Province has a drum tower and that they differ from one another only in size and date of construction. We thought back on all the towns we had passed and realized that he was right. In the Hexi area even Yongchang, a tiny town, has a drum tower very much like the one in Jiuquan, although the former is much smaller in size.

Ancient Waterwheels on the Yellow River

By evening we had arrived at Mojialou in Zhongwei County, Ningxia. A vehicular ferry took us across the still and peaceful Yellow River. The water in this part of the river was beginning to take on a yellowish colour, but was much clearer than the muddier sections which flow through the Shaanxi-Shanxi Canyon and other places in Henan and Shandong provinces. The sun was already setting when our car passed Zhongwei. We could not afford to stop, so we rushed across town and headed straight for Shapotou, a town nearby. It was

清真饭馆
羊肉泡馍
羊肉稍子面
羊肉手揪面
羊肉拌面
刀削炒面
八宝盖碗茶
米饭炒菜
凉菜拼盘

One side of Little Tian'anmen's reviewing stand has been turned into a mutton restaurant.

already dark when we got to the Desert Research Institute, where we were to stay the night.

At 7 a.m. the next day we took a drive to see some sand dunes nearby. Soon the sun was shining on the great Yellow River, whose banks had been turned into fertile paddy fields. Beyond the river's northern bank lies the Tengger Desert, a vast expanse of land more than 40,000 square kilometres in size. For years clouds of sand used to blow in from the desert in the north, burying numerous villages and fields. In the end the local residents realized that they had no alternative but to fight for their survival. In 1958 a research institute was established at Shapotou, subsequently becoming very successful in bringing the desert under control.

The gently flowing Yellow River in Ningxia suddenly surges ahead once it enters the valley between Shaanxi and Shanxi.

Shapotou now claims to be a very popular desert sightseeing spot in Ningxia. Tourists who come here can not only see the desert and the Yellow River, but can also ride in a sheep-skin raft on the river, or ride horses or camels to simulate the desert expeditions of old.

The man who rents in the sheep-skin raft told us that the village was named Shapotou and that the village on the southern bank of the river was called Waterwheel Village, where a few Yellow River waterwheels still remained. We ferried across the river and spotted the wreckage of two waterwheels. Although no longer in use, the waterwheels are still a reminder of the supreme and mighty power they wielded in their heyday, with their giant skeletons rising high on the vast open spaces of the banks.

Entering Waterwheel Village, we were told by the villagers that the waterwheels had fallen into disuse over a dozen years ago. While the other waterwheels along the river had already been dismantled, the two remaining ones in their village were saved from total destruction due to the timely intervention of the county's bureau of tourism, which also hired an old keeper to guard the waterwheels.

The Renovation of 108 Pagodas

It was not until 3:00 in the afternoon that we at last had our first meal of the day. We returned to Zhongwei, where we had planned to take a walk and look around the town, but as soon as we got out of the car a yellow cloud of sand blew in our

faces and it immediately started to rain. The only thing we could do was to get back into our car and to drive on towards Qingtongxia, about halfway to our destination of Yinchuan. We stayed overnight in Qingtongxia and the next morning decided to pay a visit to the Qingtongxia Reservoir, near which are 108 pagodas that we wanted to see.

At the reservoir we boarded a tourist boat which took us to the other side in a few minutes. The pagodas had all been renovated, resulting in a completely new look. From records on the renovation work, we learnt that the renovation was actually a kind of "restoration" done by peeling off the layers of plaster that had been added over several dynasties. The result revealed the pagodas' original style, that of the Song Dynasty (960-1279).

Apart from its pagodas, Qingtongxia is also

The sheep-skin raft is a traditional means of crossing the Yellow River.

renowned for its 44 temples located in Niushou (Ox Head) Mountain, plus its prairies, forests and vast expanses of reed marshes. As we had planned to cover a long distance within a limited time, we were obliged to skip these scenic wonders and continue our journey north.

The Haibao Pagoda and the Sand Lake

Wherever we went during our journey, it seemed we were always climbing either towers or pagodas, as if Chinese culture had been concentrated in this one region. On the following day, we continued our cultural tour and rode to the northern suburbs to visit Haibao Pagoda. This nine-storey pagoda is 54 metres in height and has quite an extraordinary design. If it were cut in half down the middle, it would reveal a cross-section that resembles the Chinese character " 亞 ". The pagoda, overlooks the vast Yinchuan Plain at the Great Bend of the Yellow River with the undulating Helan Mountains stretching out in the west. The mountains were clad in delicate blue and purple shades, with not a single inch of greenness anywhere.

That afternoon we took another tour with some friends to Shahu (Sand Lake), situated more than 30 kilometres northwest of Yinchuan's old city. When we arrived we found that the place truly did deserve its name. Tourists were making their way in boats through the labyrinth of 72 lakes by detouring around one sand hill after another. Suddenly it began to pour and our boat darted through the reeds and sand hills to hurry back to

The old city area
of Yinchuan.

shore.

Fortresses Now in Ruins

Accompanied by friends we set out early the next morning to see the rock paintings at the Helan Mountain Pass. We left the old city and after a long ride on a country road, arrived at an urban area. We drove across the new city into a wilderness of rocks and wasteland, where there were few people and little cultivation. The far-away Qilian Mountains could still be seen at twilight. Before long we spotted a dilapidated earth fortress to the right of the highway. We turned off the highway and after several detours drove into a fortified town, which

The double-tower located at the east foot of the Helan Mountain is the relic of the Western Xia Kingdom.

seemed somehow oddly familiar.

It turned out that this was none other than the exterior shooting location for the Chinese movie *Red Sorghum*. When we came out of the town we saw an even larger and more well-preserved fortress lying not far off to the north, which was the well-known Zhenbei Fortress.

Although perilous and precipitous, throughout history the Helan Mountains have been accessible via many mountain passes, which had to be guarded and protected. In order to prevent intrusion, the emperors of the Ming Dynasty had a number of fortresses built at each mountain pass. These fortresses were inhabited by soldiers who, on spotting the enemy troops, would light up smoke signals and assemble for the fight. Hundreds of years have passed since then, and these fortresses, no longer in use, have gradually fallen into ruin. The size of a small town in ancient times, the fortress could have accommodated an entire

Western Xia attached importance to assimilating the advanced Han culture, the characters of Western Xia referred to the Chinese characters. These are Western Xia scripture types for printing.

regiment of soldiers.

Zhenbei Fortress has only one gate, which is in the middle of the eastern wall with the Helan Mountains towering behind. As we were approaching the gate, we spotted a smaller building outside. We went in and were immediately overcome by a heavy odour of sheep. It turned out that this part of the fortress had been converted into an enormous sheepfold.

Rock Paintings and Inscriptions from the Western Xia

By 9:00 in the morning we had arrived at the Helan Mountain. On either side the hills were barren except for rocks and weeds. The so-called Helan rock paintings were found in this area, known for their frank and somewhat primitive depictions of the daily activities of an ancient nomadic tribe. The paintings show people hunting, playing games, farming and even performing sexual intercourse. Simple and concise, the paintings have an artistic and aesthetic appeal all their own.

We also saw carved inscriptions written in Western Xia characters. The Western Xia Kingdom had no written language, and the Western Xia people adopted the basic structure of Han Chinese characters. Halfway up a hill along the Helan Mountain we also found paintings of humans, either with two horns on their head or with a face that resembled a sunflower. These were done at the same time as the other paintings, and represented

two images of gods worshipped by these farming people.

The Looted and Pillaged Western Xia Imperial Tombs

Our next stop was to visit the Western Xia Imperial Tombs, which are situated on a wasteland next to the Helan Mountains, 25 kilometres away from the urban area of Yinchuan. The tombs stretch along the mountain slope from south to north for 14 kilometres. The main tombs are the

resting places of nine emperors, and there are also more than 70 other tombs belonging to empresses, princes, princesses, courtiers and warriors.

We then visited the mausoleum of Li Yuanhao, the first emperor of the Western Xia Dynasty. Imperial tombs of the Western Xia are different from those of Han kingdoms, in that the tomb room is built not under a dome but under and in front of the projecting mourning table. The tombs of Li Yuanhao and his successors were unfortunately all dug up and looted by conquerors of the Yuan Dynasty. The surrounding palaces, towers, buildings and pavilions have also been burnt down, and today all that remains are some dilapidated walls and solitary mourning tables.

The mourning tables were the most conspicuous because of their size and height. In the distance they looked like haystacks commonly seen in the countryside south of the Yangtse River. We were told that originally each clay mourning table was enclosed by a wooden pagoda five or seven storeys high in the shape of an octahedron.

Towards the end of Western Xia Dynasty, Genghis Khan launched five fierce attacks on the Western Xia, only to find his armies suffering heavy losses and himself wounded by a poisoned arrow. Before his death he gave an order that all the members of Li's royal family be killed and the city be destroyed following the defeat of the Western Xia.

Later Genghis Khan's son and successor launched the sixth attack, which eventually led to the fall of this kingdom. The conqueror

The Western Xia mausoleum is standing silently at the eastern foot of the Helan Mountain. It is an embodiment of the long-vanished Western Xia culture.

Zhenbei Fortress,
built in the Ming
Dynasty as a military
fortification against
the Mongols, today
serves as a sheepfold.

then ordered a deliberate, total destruction of the Western Xia Imperial Tombs to avenge the death of his emperor father. The treasures buried underground were dug up and taken away, the buildings all burnt down and the stelae that recorded the achievements of Western Xia emperors smashed to pieces.

All this occurred decades before Marco Polo passed through this region. At that time the area from the Helan Mountains extending to both sides of the Yellow River was under the control of the Mongolian armies.

Meeting a Caliph

The next day we went to visit a village named Najiahu in Yongning County, which is located to the south of Yinchuan. The inhabitants here are nearly all Muslims. Before we arrived at the village, we saw in the distance a dignified-looking mosque. To its left stood a tall Wangyue (Moon Viewing) Tower, very much like the gun tower that protected the premises of a rich Han family in those days. However, we soon recognized the Islamic symbol of a crescent moon and star on top of the tower.

We went in through the gate and saw a spacious courtyard, on both sides of which were rows of rooms serving as dormitories for the chief imam and his students. Opposite the gate across the courtyard was the prayer hall. In front and on each side of the prayer hall were massive, sturdy, antique Chinese scholartrees.

In appearance the buildings we saw were in

typical Han-style architecture. But once inside, we saw that the entire interior was decorated according to Islamic style. The prayer hall, where carpets were spread wall to wall, was enormous: over 1,000 faithful could kneel in prayer at one time. Behind the dormitory rooms on the left was a bathing hall, which was paved with patterned bricks and included several bathing pools and bathtubs.

The Sunni mosque at Najiahu Village is quite well known in Ningxia.

In the reception room we met Murshid Ma, caliph (a Muslim ruler) of the Najiahu Mosque. He was already 91 but could still hear and see well and think fast. He told us, very proudly, that he had gone on a pilgrimage to Mecca the previous year with the help of his son. He said that any Muslim, not only caliphs, would feel very honored if they had the opportunity to make a pilgrimage to Mecca.

Home of Nescradin, a Famous General

Mr. Ma also related to us the village's history.

A screen wall is being built at the mosque at Najiahu Village.

According to him, there was a general named Nescradin in the Yuan Dynasty who fought against Burma king and later was bestowed by Genghis Khan with a piece of land in Ningxia for his meritorious service. Nescradin had many children and grandchildren who wanted to conform to Han custom, therefore they divided his name into Na, Su, La and Ding to make four Chinese surnames. This is why Ningxia has a village called Najiahu (Na family residence) and Xi'an has a village called Lajiacun (La family village).

Today it is the Na family in Ningxia that claims to be the most populous, with over 4,000 residents in the village of Najiahu. Ninety-seven per cent of them are Muslims and over half of them are descendants of Nescradin. In *The Travels*, Marco Polo gives a detailed account of General Nescradin's battle in 1272 against the armies of the King of Mien (Myanmar), whose territories Kublai Khan later conquered. Thus Mescradin and Marco

Polo were contemporaries, and perhaps had even made one another's acquaintance.

Mr. Ma also told us that Muslims at Najiahu belong to the Sunni sect, whose caliphs are elected, rather than designated, as is the practice with other Islamic sects. When asked about the special products in Ningxia, the old man became enthusiastic. He recommended *tanyang* (sands sheep) skin, Chinese wolfberry fruit, *fa* tea, licorice root and Helan rocks. He also recommended Ningxia mutton, which he said was the best mutton under the sun. He believed that mutton hot-pot actually originated in his hometown.

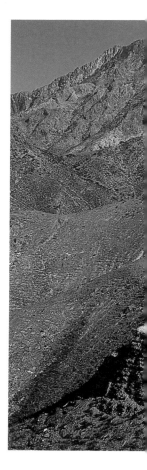

Having said goodbye to our Muslim friends in Najiahu, we headed straight for Shuidonggou, where relics of the Palaeolithic Era have been discovered. It stands on the banks of a Yellow River tributary, close to the ruins and signal towers of the Great Wall.

We left Shuidonggou and arrived at the foot of the Great Wall near Hengcheng Fort. As I was climbing the dilapidated wall battlements, my foot hit a round object. I bent over and picked it up and found that it was an ancient coin. We examined the coin in turn and could only recognize three Chinese characters: Sheng, Yuan and Bao. The fourth character was unidentifiable. Back at Yinchuan that night, we located an illustrated book on numismatics at a friend's house and learnt that the four Chinese characters were: *Shao Sheng* (the title of Emperor Zhezong) *Yuan Bao* (money). This meant that the coin was issued in the Northern Song period when Emperor Zhezong

The Sanguankou Great Wall at the pass of the Helan Mountain. Passing this mountain pass, you will enter the Alxa area.

reigned (1086-1100).

Across the Helan Mountains

The next day we got up early in the morning and left Yinchuan while it was still dark. We drove across the old city and then across the new urban area. When the sun was about to shed its first rays of light on the earth we again passed the Western Xia Imperial Tombs. The undulating Helan Mountains stretched from north to south, as bare and plain as ever. At about 9:00 we found ourselves

once more in the canyons of the Helan Mountains.

In ancient times the Helan Mountains were considered an excellent natural barrier. The Han regimes had always made use of this fact, with the help of the Great Wall, to repulse the invading marauders of the non-Han nationalities, However, in present-day military affairs, the Helan Mountains are of no more importance than a small hill.

On our last day in this region we crossed the Helan Mountain Pass and entered Inner Mongolia. Although we had been driving for only an hour, we noticed that the vegetation and the geographic features on the western slopes of Inner Mongolia were completely different from those on the eastern slopes in Ningxia. All around one could see a vast expanse of desert and prairie, boundless and smooth. There was little livestock except for a few camels, cattle and sheep roaming about in the wilderness. It was 11:00 in the morning when we arrived at our next destination, Alxa Left Banner (Bayan Hot), capital of Alxa League in Inner Mongolia.

A Detour Through the Desert to Etzina

苏吉诺尔
Sogo Nur

额济纳旗
Ejin Banner

黑城子
Heichengzi

乌力吉
Olji

阿拉善左旗
Alxa Left Banner

When the traveller leaves this city of Kan-chau, he rides for twelve days till he reaches a city called Etzina, which lies on the northern edge of the desert of sand. This is still in the province of Tangut. The inhabitants are idolaters. They have camels and cattle in plenty.... The people live by agriculture and stock-rearing; they are not traders.

...It is a land teeming with wild life, including wild asses, and clothed with pine-woods. There are sheets of water full of pike and other fish.

– The Travels of Marco Polo

Marco Polo's route did not actually take him directly from the Pamir Highland to Beijing, as our own journey would. In fact, he stayed for over a year in Kan-chau (Zhangye), during which he visited the ancient city of Etzina (located in today's Ejin Banner). After that, he continued north all the way through Russia and finally ended up at the Arctic Ocean. We decided to trace part of his detour as far as Ejin Banner, which required traversing yet another vast expanse of desert called the Badain Jaran.

The city Marco Polo called Kalachan was somewhere in today's Alxa League, a large area encompassing both Alxa Left Banner and Alxa Right Banner, a banner being equivalent to a county. Seven centuries ago Marco Polo saw a land full of wildlife, domestic animals, pine forests and lakes full of fish. Although one still sees camels, sheep and wild donkeys, the pine forests have long since disappeared, as have most of the bodies of water in the region. The two lakes just north of Ejin Banner shown on all maps of Inner Mongolia used to be one large lake. Today, however, one has

This little boy is standing in dried-up Sogo Nur, a sad reminder of its former glory.

The ancient city of Juyan, just beside Gaxun Nur, is now known as Heichengzi. According to Marco Polo, this desolate site was once a thriving oasis with deep water, dense forests and luxuriant grasses.

completely dried up and the other seems destined to soon follow suit.

The sculptural style of this lion in the prince's mansion is rarely seen elsewhere in China.

The last time we travelled across a desert, we suffered from intestinal and stomach troubles and our car broke down over and over again. This time, we did not dare run the risk of cutting across the Badain Jaran Desert to Ejin Banner. Instead, starting from Yinchuan we took the state road to Ejin stopping over in Alxa Left Banner (Bayan Hot), which gave us a good chance to get to know this ancient city. We were required to go through various procedures in order to get a travel permit, which was needed because our destination was quite near the Sino-Mongolian border. Therefore, we had a free afternoon in Alxa Left Banner to visit a former prince's palace, which is now a museum of history.

As we entered the palace, we suddenly felt as if we had been there before. After going round two courtyards, we found that the layout and structure of the place was exactly the same as that of the quadrangles in Beijing – walled enclosures with houses opening onto a central courtyard. The last prince of the Alxa League married a niece of Aisin Gioro Pu Yi, the last emperor of the Qing Dynasty. He often went to Beijing, and fell in love with the design of Beijing's quadrangles. He employed craftsmen from Beijing to build a quadrangle for his palace, and thereafter his subjects had their own houses built according to the prince's model. In only a couple of years, quadrangles had developed to a considerable scale, once earning Alxa Left Banner the name of "Lesser Beijing". In recent years, with the construction of new blocks, many old quadrangles have been pulled down. The remaining ones are located on a plot of land in the town centre.

On display in the main hall of the museum were traditional Mongolian clothes, weapons and articles of daily use. The curator told us that the two groups of statues, each clothed in a different style, represented the two Mongolian tribal groups living in Alxa League.

In another hall we saw an exhibition on the history of Ejin, which included objects excavated from ancient fortresses. There were clay sculptures of the Buddha made in various dynasties from the Han to the Qing, porcelain, jewelry, weapons and coins. The curator told us that the ancient city of Juyan, which flourished during the Western Han

Dynasty, is located in Ejin Banner and is now called Heichengzi. The ruins of beacon towers and the Great Wall run along a 200-kilometre-long stretch of desert, from Jinta County near Jiayuguan in Gansu Province to Ejin, In particular, many precious historical relics have been excavated from the large-scale ruins of Heichengzi at the northernmost end of this stretch.

After our visit at the museum over, we left the downtown area and went northwest to visit the Alxa League Camel Hair Cloth Mill. Marco Polo was profuse in his praise of the white camel hair cloth produced here. He wrote that it was exported by merchants far and wide to many countries,

Judging from the thickness of the remaining walls, one can imagine the magnificence and prosperity of Heichengzi in its heyday.

including Khitan. All the work in this mill is done by machine. In the exhibition room, we saw camel hair sweaters in various styles, and also camel hair cloth, which most likely is the curiously-named "camlets" described in his book.

Another Day in the Desert

At noon the next day (Sep. 2nd) we left "Lesser Beijing" and began our journey northward across the desert. Throughout the trip we saw endless desolate "grasslands", which despite the name held little of anything green. Instead, brownish-yellow camel thorn was thinly scattered among the dry land, which was covered in gravel. Occasionally camels in twos or threes were spotted wandering the distant desert. We were told that this was the season for herding camels, so all the domestic camels were let out to wander freely day and night on the vast grasslands. In early October, all the herdsmen would set out in search of their camels, up to one thousand in all. Each family would then claim the ones that belonged to them.

The further we went, the worse the road became. Not only was it bumpy, but the road was also coated with sand nearly 20 centimetres thick, which enveloped our car as it sped ahead. Fortunately, the continuously heavy winds blew the dust across our car, driving away the worst of it. From time to time, our car would pass by the edge of the Tengger Desert. After several hours of bumping along on the dry and windy plateau, we saw a yurt and a couple of houses which belonged to a road

maintenance crew. The houses stood out against the vast, gently undulating land, the tallest structures to be seen for miles.

We continued driving and at last saw an oasis, where there were short trees and houses built of mud-bricks. Farmers were gathering in their crops, so we stopped to have a chat with them. It turned out that they were immigrants from Minqin County in Gansu Province. They had settled here for nearly 20 years, as there was more farmable land than in their hometown.

Beyond the oasis, it was again a seemingly endless road through the desert. The dry, hot wind cracked our lips. We continually ate fruit and had drinks, but they did not help much. Towards sunset, our car arrived at a town called Oiji. At the frontier inspection station we showed our travel permits, as is required of all cars and passengers going to Ejin. That evening we put up at a hostel in the town, still one more day's journey away from Ejin.

Along the Sino-Mongolian Border

The next day was spent travelling along the Sino-Mongolian border, an area even more desolate than our journey the day before. The land lacked even dry creepers, let alone trees.

Our two-day, 780-kilometre ride in the desert was finally at an end. We wondered if Marco Pole had the same feeling of relief when he arrived at this oasis town after his long desert journey. The road to Ejin was lined with trees, whose leaves

Ejin is known as China's "home of camels".

were turning yellow in the autumn air. While enjoying the beautiful scenery, all at once we found ourselves in the downtown area.

Early the next morning, we drove into a forest at the end of the Ejin River Valley and came to an area of flowering willow bushes. The light, purplish-red flowers were in bloom and our car was surrounded by shrubs in all directions. Paths crisscrossed the clumps of bushes, causing our driver to become first puzzled and then helplessly lost. After making several turns we found ourselves back in the forest, and declared that from then on we would ask directions whenever we passed by a house. After another hour of turning about in the maze-like forest, we finally found our way out and continued on, soon coming to a dry river valley.

Along the banks of the river, the stumps of long-

dead trees stood miserably on mounds, looking like a scene from the desolate landscapes of Qinghai. Suddenly, our car was overtaken by two jeeps, which we followed and used as a guide, preventing us from getting lost again in this eerie river valley.

Heichengzi – the Ruins of an Ancient City

Our car drove south for a while, then left the dry riverbed and approached the edge of a desert. Between the riverbed and the desert stood the ruins of an ancient city. Although the top and some parts of the city walls had collapsed, the city was still intact on the whole. This was the place that we had travelled some 700 kilometres to see – the location of the ancient city of Juyan.

What is now known as Heichengzi (Black City) was built during the Western Xia Kingdom. According to historical records, a thousand years before that, Emperor Wudi (r. 140-87 B.C.) of the Western Han Dynasty sent troops here to farm and defend this area, where the northern part of the Han Dynasty Great Wall ended. According to legend, much later Heichengzi was defended by a troop commanded by a general whose nick-name was Hei (Black). While under his command, enemy troops attacked the city but failed because it was so solid and strongly fortified. Therefore the enemy turned to cutting off the water supply by stopping the flow of the Ejin River into the city.

Seeing that the water was running out and that his troops might not be able to hold out much

longer, General Hei ordered his soldiers to hide all the city's treasures in a dried-up well and then tried to fight his way out, but was killed in action. Later the enemy troops captured the city and killed all its citizens and the remaining soldiers. However the enemy troops failed to find the treasure, and ever since then only the ruins of the city have remained.

Hunting for Buried Treasure

The legend about the hidden treasure has, not surprisingly, attracted many treasure hunters. Heichengzi is famous in archaeological circles because so many historical relics have been discovered here during treasure hunts. In modern times, many foreign expeditions have been to Heichengzi, among them the Russian officer P. K. Kozlov and the British "Robber of Cultural Relics" Mark Aurel Stein. They dug everywhere in the

Camels are left free to graze on the grassland.

ruins to search for the treasure hidden by General Hei.

For two days and one night we drove along this seemingly endless desert road.

They never found the well but did unearth many rare sutras, documents and other relics from the Western Xia Kingdom and the Yuan Dynasty. They took away all their finds without any hesitation, and these objects are now kept in museums in Russia and Britain. Although the ancient city is now desolate and in ruins, it still attracts the attention of both archaeologists and tourists.

With great effort, we climbed the sand dunes and mounted the city wall, which was half buried by sand. In the bright sunshine, we could just make out the layout of the old city. It had been built in a rectangle and was two kilometres wide. In the middle of the east and west city walls were city gates, outside of which further walls were built to help in defence. However, the gateways had long been blocked up by sand, so we had to climb over the city wall to enter the city. Tempted by the lure of

The herdsmen enjoying their work and life in the Etzina Oasis.

buried riches, we looked everywhere, hoping that we might chance on some remains of the treasure. We walked around and were able to roughly figure out the patterns of ancient streets and broken mud-brick walls. Eaves and pillars in alignment pierced through the drifting sand, indicating that the city had flourished in ancient times.

In fact, there were indeed quite a lot of historical relics still around. In less than an hour, our hands and pockets were full of fragments of Yuan Dynasty celadon, black porcelain and blue and white pottery. We also unearthed a lady's leather boot and an incomplete Yuan coin. In the southern corner of the city, we saw red clay that had been fired at high temperatures and many pieces of broken earthenware. We gathered that there must have been a pottery and porcelain workshop here at one time.

Near Heichengzi, there is an area 40 kilometres long and 25 kilometres wide called the "secret and

The expedition headed by Kozlof came to Sichuan by way of Mongolia. When passing by Etzina area, they encountered Hichengzi.

mysterious black sand hills". Even local herdsmen get lost among these hills. In winter and spring when fierce winds blow, sand flies about and stones hurtle through the air, while sand hills shift constantly. Broken walls poke out of the sand, and some people have even glimpsed the roofs of ancient temples. Because it is so treacherous, very little is known about this unique place.

The Story of the Vanishing Lakes

When we were in Zhangye we consulted a map and saw that the Ruoshui River has its source in the Qilian Mountains, then winds north through the Hexi Corridor and into the desert. It then flows through the forests of Ejin Banner and pours into two lakes – the Gaxun Nur and the Sogo Nur.

The next morning we drove again towards the Sino-Mongolian border.

Next, we headed northeast to visit Sogo Nur. After two hours of driving through low willow bushes, we saw the white surface of a lake. A solitary thatched cottage stood by the road leading to the lake, and the sound of our engine brought a

middle-aged Mongolian man out to greet us. After a short conversation our Mongolian guide told us that the lake had dried up just ten days earlier. However, we refused to believe him and decided to go there to see the lake with our own eyes. What we saw was an endless stretch of cracked earth, the bottom of the lake, which was covered with a coating of frostlike powder that looked like salinealkali.

Suddenly, a vast stretch of water appeared in the distance. Our Mongolian guide thought it might be the remaining water in the lake. We drove on for a couple of kilometres only to find that the water surface disappeared before our very eyes. Then when we looked back again, we saw a stretch of water appear where we had just stopped. It was not water at all but a mirage, playing a trick on our eyes.

The ground at Heichengzi has been dug up numerous times by treasure hunters over the past 200 years.

This dead stump of an ancient
diversiform-leaved poplar
tree has borne witness to the
vicissitudes of history, and
perhaps was here even in
Marco Polo's time.

A Happy Township on the Grassland

Early the next morning we arrived in Jirigelantu Sumu. In Mongol this means "happy township", and the name does the town justice. Tall, thick trees joined together to shade the ground from the scorching sun. Mongolian families lived scattered under the trees. In places where there are no trees, a kind of purplish-red grass grows, which takes on a red colour quite pleasing to the eye in the morning sun, looking like a plush carpet in a fine hotel. The leaves of the plant were actually translucent stems

containing a red juice. Unfortunately, we were unable to classify this lovely plant.

We entered a yurt whose dwellers are an old couple.

The couple were both over 70 and seemed very friendly. The old woman served us hot milk tea, which we had drunk daily since we entered Inner Mongolia. The tea is made by first brewing black tea, adding a pinch of salt and then adding some fresh goat milk or cow milk. When we first tasted the tea, we were not used to it and found it undrinkable. We thought it was interesting that just two days later, we came to savour the taste and could not do without it.

When our cups of milk tea were finished, the old man untied the snuff bottle hanging at his waist and handed it to us for a sniff. We had only read about this in novels and had never had the experience of actually using snuff. With great care and imitating the old man's example, one person in our party decided to give it a try. She wiped the mouth of the bottle with her thumb, then put the bottle to her nostril and sniffed three times. Suddenly she dashed out of the yurt and sneezed violently until she felt normal again.

The herdsmen cherish their plain-coloured snuff bottles, and always wear them at their waist. When Mongolian men meet, they give each other a sniff out of their snuff bottle. Offering the snuff bottle is also a Mongolian courtesy to express respect and good will to guests from afar.

We were interested to see that almost all the tools here were made of wood from a local species of

In the surburbs of Ejin Banner there is a vast stretch of grassland that looks like a plush red carpet.

diversiform-leaved poplar tree. In addition to the fences, pails of all sizes, grain storage tanks, tables, stools, cupboards, chests and kitchen utensils were all made of this same wood. One special feature of these homemade utensils was that all the round ones were made by hollowing-out logs of various diameters, giving the objects a natural beauty.

Mongolian yurts are always colourfully furnished.

As we were about to bid our farewell, the old man told us a valuable piece of information: a herdsman living not far away was going to hold a ceremony that day to have his son's hair cut, and the old woman in the family was going there. It seemed like a good opportunity, so we brought her along as our guide to ensure that we would not get lost.

A Mongolian Hair-Cutting Ceremony

Along the way we met Mongolians of all ages riding on donkeys and motorcycles in the same

direction as ours. Apparently, they were also going to attend the hair-cutting ceremony. When we arrived, everyone was gathered in an open area in front of two yurts and two mud-brick houses. Both animals and vehicles pulled up outside the fence, the passengers dressed in traditional Mongolian outfits. Carrying various gifts, everyone was invited into the yurt.

The hair-cutting ceremony is to the Mongolians what baptism is to Christians. The hair of all Mongolian babies, boys and girls alike, has to be allowed to grow until the boy is three and the girl is four. Then an auspicious day is chosen for a grand hair-cutting ceremony, with all the relatives and friends attending. The ceremony is a milestone, showing that the baby has reached this particular age.

The yurt was crowded with people who were sitting in two rows, males on the left and females

The hair-cutting ceremony performed on all Mongolian children is as important as baptism is for Christians.

on the right. The boy's father made an opening speech expressing his welcome and gratitude to the guests. Then a Mongolian girl came in, carrying a tray and holding a pair of scissors. The oldest and most prestigious guest made the first cut, which was followed by everyone in turn, each cutting off a piece of hair. When the baby's hair was all cut, the host treated the guests to mutton, snacks, milk tea, cheese and fruit milk. He proposed a toast to each of his guests, one after the other. The wine was translucent, and when we drank some we found that it was neither spirit nor wine. We were told it was "milk wine" made from mare's milk.

The "wine" had gone round three times and the guests became less reserved. They began singing beautiful folk songs of blessing and praise, leaving us with yet more unforgettable memories of this ancient and mysterious land.

THE ANCIENT ORDOS PLATEAU

乌力吉
Olji

呼和浩特
Hohhot

吉兰泰
Jartai

东胜
Dongsheng

准格尔旗
Jungar Banner

石嘴山
Shizuishan

成吉思汗陵
Genghis Khan
Mausoleum

松树塲
Pine Hill

Now it happened in the year of ... 1187 ... the Tartars chose a king to reign over them whose name in their language was Chinghiz Khan, a man of great ability and wisdom, a gifted orator and a brilliant soldier. After his election, all the Tartars in the world, dispersed as they were among various foreign countries, come to him and acknowledged his sovereignty. And he exercised it well and honourably ... so that he was loved and honoured not as a lord but as a god.

... All the great lords who are of the lineage of Chinghiz Khan are conveyed for burial to a great mountain called Altai. When one of them dies, even if it be at a distance of a hundred days' journey from this mountain, he must be brought here for burial.

– The Travels of Marco Polo

A lthough not entirely planned, this part of
our journey brought us to the Genghis
(Chinghiz) Khan Mausoleum, located in
Ejin Horo Banner in Inner Mongolia. Although
it is possible that Maroo Polo's account of where
Genghis Khan and his descendants are buried is
true, no evidence of this has ever been discovered,
nor have their tombs ever been found. The
mausoleum we visited, therefore, did not contain
the remains of the emperor, but was rather a
memorial hall.

Marco Polo devoted a fair amount of space in

his book in praise of Genghis Khan, although by today's standards he would hardly be considered a benevolent leader. For example, Marco Polo tells us that when Genghis Khan or one of his successors died and was being taken for burial, "all those who are encountered along the route... are put to the sword by the attendants who are escorting it." This was because it was believed that all these people would be there to serve the emperor after death. When Genghis Khan's grandson Mongu Khan died in 1259, over 20,000 people were put to death in this way.

Genghis Khan is perhaps buried somewhere on the vast Ordos Plateau.

We left the beautiful oasis of Ejin Banner and continued our journey eastward. We planned to cover 600 kilometres in a day in order to reach Linhe, a town north of Yinchuan along the Yellow River. On the way, we came across a lone courtyard surrounded on all sides by the vast desert. On its outer wall was a slogan in big Chinese characters reading "Highway 401 Maintenance Crew, a Forgotten Paradise." Well, perhaps it was a paradise once, but no longer. Looking around, one sees no greenery, no lakes or rivers and very few birds or animals. The road past it was like a single reef in an immense ocean. Only two or three workers in charge of maintaining the dirt highway stay here all year round, no doubt a hard and lonely life.

We soon reached Oiji, a small town on the border with Mongolia. From here, we turned south and headed for Linhe. The scenery changed as grass, yurts and elm trees on both sides of the road came into sight. Horses, camels and flocks of sheep freely roamed on the grassland.

的天堂"罗道班"

A highway maintenance
crew are the only people,
besides ourselves, on this
long desert road.

Going to Jartai by Mistake

The people in this village had a bumper harvest this year.

It was getting dark, but our odometer showed that we were near our destination. The further we drove, the more grass there was, sometimes even growing on the highway. Under the glare of the car's headlamps, it looked unusually green. At last, we saw lights up ahead and stopped our car to make inquiries. We were told that in fact this was not Linhe but Jartai, a name entirely unfamiliar to us.

We looked at our map against the light of the headlamps and discovered, to our dismay, that we had taken a wrong turn. We should have continued going eastward until we reached Linhe, but instead we had made the mistake of turning south at a crossing and were now more than 200 kilometres south of our destination! We had to change our

They are immigrants from Shaanxi Province. Although they have been here for decades, they still speak with a northern Shaanxi accent.

plans completely, and finally decided to head to Dongsheng, a place we were all interested in visiting. We could reach the city by driving along the road leading to Wuhai and then cross the Ordos Plateau.

Jartai, the site of China's first mechanized saltworks, is not a big town, but all its hotels were packed with tourists. We drove around the town several times and failed to find a place to put up for the night. It was by sheer luck that we met the boss of a privately-run hotel, who managed to make arrangements for our party. The next morning we took to the road again.

We crossed the Helan Mountains, passed through Wuhai and reached Shizuishan City in the northernmost part of Ningxia. At Laseng Temple, we crossed over to the east bank of the Yellow River and swung onto Highway 109 which leads to

Dongsheng, another 500 kilometres away.

A vast expanse of grassland bordered both sides of the road, however the grasses were more luxuriant on the east bank than on the west. Soon a small forest, densely-populated settlements, farmland and crops began to appear. In the evening, we passed through a village known as Sishililiangzi, where we stopped to visit some of its residents. The people here speak with a northern Shaanxi accent, as the whole village had moved here from Shenmu in Shaanxi Province. They have been engaged in farming here for more than three decades, with potatoes as their main crop.

Inhabitants of Shanxi and Shaanxi provinces migrated to the Ordos Plateau in order to make a better living. As we were approaching Dongsheng, we saw people busy doing farm work on both sides of the road. At 9:00 in the evening, we arrived at a hotel in the city.

A Modernized Genghis Khan Mausoleum

The next morning we visited the Ordos Cultural Relics Exhibition Hall, then headed for Ejin Horo Banner to have a look at the Genghis Khan Mausoleum. Along the way, two different types of terrain were visible, that of the Mongolian Plateau and the Loess Plateau. One difference is that the hills on the Loess Plateau are much steeper than that on the Mongolian Plateau, which undulates gently along the land. This is the area known as the Ordos Plateau.

The Genghis Khan Mausoleum has attracted large numbers of tourists from home and abroad in the last few years, and Ejin Horo itself has undergone great changes because of this. Its shops, hotels, restaurants and archways are all exquisitely decorated, but the mausoleum is the most magnificent structure in the city. It consists of three unoccupied round-roofed burial chambers which stand side by side, glittering against the blue sky.

The Genghis Khan Mausoleum at Ejin Horo Banner merely contains his personal effects. The question of where he was buried, however, is a riddle for centuries.

Inside, a brand-new statue of the Yuan emperor greets all visitors. Murals, painted using modern techniques, decorate the walls. Glazed porcelain pieces, ornate lamps, marble pillars and mosaic tiles all add to the grandeur of the place. Unfortunately,

none of it has retained, or attempted to recreate, the artistic style of the Yuan Dynasty. Instead, it is clearly a product of today's craftsmen.

According to experts at the Dongsheng Museum, Mongolian emperors were buried secretly after their death. Their coffins, like those used today by Ejin Banner herdsmen, were the hollowed-out trunks of trees. Their remains were buried either in an ancestral ground or in a spot the deceased emperor had favoured during his lifetime. After the burial, the ground was trampled down by thousands of galloping horses and turned into a hard, level surface. Then the emperor's most faithful soldiers were sent to guard the site until it was overgrown with grass. The burial ground gradually became part of the grassland over the years, so that no one would be able to tell its exact location. After many years of painstaking conjecture, searching and digging, no trace of his grave has been found. It is still a mystery.

The Yuan-Dynasty porcelain assimilated the characters of both the Song-Dynasty and the Islamic porcelain arts to create many new types such as blue and white porcelain with underglaze red, porcelain with cobalt blue glaze and porcelain with rouge blambe. So that the three-thousand-year celadon time ended, the porcelain art hit a new peak.

An Old Village and a Mystical Tree

We left Dongsheng in the morning and headed south to visit a famous temple called Jungar, about 40 kilometres away from Dongsheng. The minute we arrived in the village where the temple was,

we noticed it had an ancient air about it, with few of the modern touches we had seen elsewhere. Its houses and courtyards have a history dating back 100 years, and the halls of the temple were even older. The bricks and tiles were exquisitely engraved, and the doors and window frames, though old or broken, were carved with beautiful patterns.

Inside the houses were large wooden cabinets painted in red, with brass decorations perhaps 50 or 60 years old. Almost all the villagers are Mongolians, but they speak Mandarin fluently, since the area is also inhabited by Han Chinese. In addition, immigrants from northern Shaanxi have had a great impact on the people here, which explains why the Mongolians in the village have taken up farming.

This is an exterior of the movie *Marco Polo* joint-shot by China and Italy, which was later called "The Temporary Dwelling Palace of Genghis Khan" and became a tourist attraction.

After leaving the Jungar Temple, we took an
unfamiliar and rather dangerous road in search of
"the king of the Chinese pine" in northern China.
This sole tree is on a hill in the Jungar highland,
and there is virtually no road leading to it. We
first drove along the riverbed and then up a hill,
following the ditches scoured out by the rain. The
ridge of the hill was flanked by deep valleys and
ahead of it were steep slopes. Many a time we felt
that our search was hopeless, but there was no
retreat, since it was impossible for the car to turn
around on the treacherous path.

All we could do was forge ahead, when all of
a sudden the car went stumbling downhill. In
the deep loess canyons on both sides of the ridge,

This solitary 900-year-
old Chinese pine still
stands on a hill in the
Loess Plateau.

strong winds howled and eagles hovered in the air while our car took a downward plunge. We felt dizzy with fear, and it took us more than five hours to cover a distance of less than 100 kilometres. Dusk came, and at last we caught sight of the mystical tree standing alone on a hill against the setting sun.

The place, called Pine Hill, is known for this towering tree which, though more than 900 years old, still flourishes here. In the eyes of many people, it is no ordinary plant but a mystical tree, and it attracts many worshippers. A monastery has now been built around the tree, and on July 15 of every

It was a bumper harvest this autumn, the fruits of which will carry these people through the long winter months.

year a temple fair is held here, during which
people living within a radius of several
hundred kilometres come to pay homage.

We left the tree and descended the hill. In

China's Loess Plateau
spreads out over
Shaanxi, Shanxi,
Gansu and Ningxia.

the twilight, we saw some cave dwellings on the slope, looking even more primitive than those in northern Shaanxi. At night, we arrived in Jungar Banner.

Coalfields on the Border

We crossed the Yellow River at Lamawan and drove north on the highway along the river. All the way, we passed truck after truck laden with coal. In the last few years, a large open-cut coal mine has been built on the border area between Shanxi and Inner Mongolia. The coal is abundant and of high quality, so the prospects for the mine are quite good.

In his book, Marco Polo also mentioned seeing coal in China. He wrote, "It is a fact that throughout the province of Cathay there is a sort of black stone, which is dug out of veins in the hillsides and burns like logs. These stones keep a fire going better than wood. I assure you that, if you put them on the fire in the evening and see that they are well alight, they will continue to burn all night, so that you will find them still glowing in the morning." From this account one can see that at the time, coal had not yet been discovered in Europe. The Chinese seem to have been using coal as fuel many years before Europeans and people elsewhere.

Very soon, we came to a plain at the Great Bend of the Yellow River. The local people call the area the Rear Great Bend to distinguish it from the Great Bend in Ningxia. The fertile plain looked endless, continuing right up to Hohhot. Both sides of the road were covered with dense forests, whose leaves were beginning to turn yellow. We had begun our journey in the Pamir Highland in mid-summer, and now it was already late autumn.

VISITING THE YUAN CAPITALS OF SHANG-TU AND KHAN-BALIK

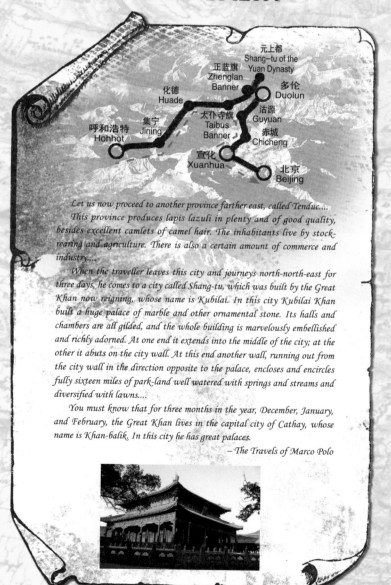

元上都
Shang-tu of the
Yuan Dynasty

正蓝旗
Zhenglan
Banner

多伦
Duolun

化德
Huade

太仆寺旗
Taibus
Banner

沽源
Guyuan

集宁
Jining

赤城
Chicheng

呼和浩特
Hohhot

宣化
Xuanhua

北京
Beijing

Let us now proceed to another province farther east, called Tenduc....

This province produces lapis lazuli in plenty and of good quality, besides excellent camlets of camel hair. The inhabitants live by stock-rearing and agriculture. There is also a certain amount of commerce and industry....

When the traveller leaves this city and journeys north-north-east for three days, he comes to a city called Shang-tu, which was built by the Great Khan now reigning, whose name is Kubilai. In this city Kubilai Khan built a huge palace of marble and other ornamental stone. Its halls and chambers are all gilded, and the whole building is marvelously embellished and richly adorned. At one end it extends into the middle of the city; at the other it abuts on the city wall. At this end another wall, running out from the city wall in the direction opposite to the palace, encloses and encircles fully sixteen miles of park-land well watered with springs and streams and diversified with lawns....

You must know that for three months in the year, December, January, and February, the Great Khan lives in the capital city of Cathay, whose name is Khan-balik. In this city he has great palaces.

— The Travels of Marco Polo

The temporary palace of Empress Dowager Xiao of the Liao Dynasty still stands in Guyuan County, Hebei.

top left: What used to be pasture land is now being brought under cultivation.

bottom left: A beautiful view of farmland in autumn.

The province referred to by Marco Polo as Tenduc is the region north of the Great Wall around Hohhot in Inner Mongolia's Xulun Hoh Banner. The ruins of the Great Khan's magnificent palace in Shang-tu, where Marco Polo was received by Kublai Khan, have been discovered, but there is little left except rubble and some remains of the city walls.

Marco Polo wrote, "The Great Khan stays at Shang-tu for three months in the year, June, July and August, to escape from the heat and for the sake of the recreation it affords." This tradition of emperors and empresses having a summer residence to escape the heat of the capital had been handed down over the dynasties, and continued until the Qing Dynasty with the Empress Dowager Cixi's famous Summer Palace.

Even more grand than Shang-tu, the first capital, was the Yuan Dynasty's Great Capital at Khan-balik, today's Beijing. According to Marco Polo, the Mongolian name of Khan-balik meant "the Lord's city", and was also called Taidu at that time. About this ancient capital he wrote, "The city is full of fine mansions, inns and dwelling-houses." Marco Polo

stayed as Kublai Khan's guest at Khan-balik off and on for the next 17 years, making excursions into uncharted territories for the ever-curious ruler.

We arrived in Beijing, our last stop, in October, the same time of year that Marco Polo first entered the city.

Marco Polo left the province of Egrigaia (present-day Ningxia), and arrived at Tenduc, the capital city of Tenduc province. "This province produces... excellent camlets of camels hair. The inhabitants live by... agriculture... commerce and industry," he wrote in his book.

The ruins of the capital of Tenduc were discovered in a place called the Ancient Fengzhou Ruins east of Hohhot, the capital of the Inner Mongolia Autonomous Region. We reached Hohhot at mid-day and the next morning went to have a look at the ancient capital. The city of Tenduc has, of course, long since disappeared. Through the flat

These people have no idea that they are living within the city walls of Shang-tu, the first capital of the Yuan Dynasty.

farm fields we could faintly see what was left of the foundation of the city wall, a grass-covered ridge so low even a toddler could effortlessly climb over it.

A Pagoda Containing Yuan Relics

Towering above the fields was a white pagoda, the only ancient structure here still intact. This white pagoda enshrines Yuan Dynasty records in various written languages. Standing 40-odd metres tall, it is a seven-storey octagonal tower made of brick. Its outer walls and the colonnade of pillars on each floor are graced with sculptures of the Buddha, the Four Devarajas (Heavenly Guardians) and ferocious-looking warriors. In the gentle morning breeze the bells suspended under the roofs tinkled lightly.

Also printed during kublai khan's reign between the years 1265 and 1294, this paper money represented 500 cash.(by Chen Zhi'an)

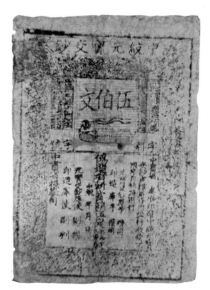

The outer walls of the pagoda are inscribed with travellers' notes dating back to the Yuan Dynasty, in Han Chinese, Mongolian, Uigur, archaic Syrian and other languages. To our great disappointment, we failed to find any travellers' notes written in Italian. These notes are proof that in ancient times, Tenduc was a transportation hub and resting place for wayfaring merchants, monks and tourists.

Recently a banknote from the Yuan Dynasty was discovered inside the pagoda. Issued during

the reign of Kublai Khan, it is believed to be the oldest banknote ever found in China. One can see the paper money on display at the museum of Hohhot.

Now in ruins, Shang-tu was once described by Marco Polo as a magnificent city.

In his book, Marco Polo gave a detailed description of the minting process used at that time: "All these papers are sealed with the seal of the Great Khan. The procedure of issue is as formal and as authoritative as if they were made of pure gold or silver. On each piece of money several specially appointed officials write their names, each setting his own stamp. When it is completed in due form, the chief of the officials deputed by the Khan dips in cinnabar the seal or bull assigned to him and stamps it on the top of the piece of money so that the shape of the seal in vermilion remains impressed upon it. And then the money is authentic. And if anyone were to forge it, he would suffer the extreme penalty."

Interestingly enough, Marco Polo also said that whenever paper money was old and damaged, it

could be brought to the mint and changed for new notes upon the payment of only three per cent. The Great Khan used the paper money in international trade and for soldiers' pay and provisions.

The Ruins of the Capital Shang-tu

We resumed our journey eastward in the morning, driving past Jining, Shangdu, Huade and Kangbao (in Hebei Province) until we arrived at Taibus Banner just access the border in Inner Mongolia. The next day we took a northeast route heading towards Xulun Hoh Banner. The land here, covered with yellow grass rustling in the high autumn wind, stretched far and wide until it reached the azure sky on the horizon. Near Shandian (Lightning) River, the mountains undulated gently, forming an imposing skyline.

Our car drove right through the city walls of what was once Shang-tu (located near present-day Duolun), the first capital of the Yuan Empire. The walls were in a shambles, but the size and shape of the colossal square enclosure were discernable from the debris and the remainder of the foundations. After comparing notes with Marco Polo's book, we learned that these were the walls of the capital's imperial palace, built of marble and other ornamental stones. The city walls were further away, now reduced to nondescript dusty ridges.

Today, what met our eyes was naked wilderness. The passage of time has laid to waste the once glorious palace of the Great Khan. Only a

The Xuanhua Catholic church built in 1900 is a typical Gothic structure.

smattering of rubble and pottery fragments stood witness to its former grandeur.

The Great Khan's Legendary Hunting Ground

It was in the city of Shang-tu that Kublai Khan received Niccolo, Maffeo and Marco Polo. It was the second time for the two older Polos to meet the Khan, but Marco's first. The Great Khan took an immediate liking to the adventurous young man and soon made him one of his attendants, with the freedom to roam about the imperial palace and beyond.

Before entering Beijing via Huailai County, we saw an ancient city named "Crowing Rooster Post Station" which looked fairly complete.

Thus the young Polo was able to visit every corner of the city of Shang-tu, a paradise surrounded by desert on all sides. In his book he rendered an exhaustive account of the imperial palace, whose majesty and splendour made him believe that he was in the most grandiose capital city in the world. However, still ahead for him was something even more remarkable, the Great Capital of the Yuan Empire in Khan-balik, today's Beijing.

On the following day we left Shang-tu and resumed our itinerary, heading southwest into Hebei Province. Taking a turn at an intersection, our car came upon what looked like a fairyland of colourful flowers and luxuriant trees.

During the Yuan Dynasty these forests, home to numerous exotic species of animals and birds, were turned into a hunting area. The Yuan emperors, de facto heads of all the nomadic tribes, were born game hunters. Marco Polo personally took part in

many hunting excursions as an attendant to Kublai Khan. In fact he devoted a large section in his book to the details of the Great Khan's hunting activities, which usually involved a 10,000-strong retinue in tow plus as many gerfalcons and hawks as he liked. This was also an imperial hunting ground for the emperors of the Qing Dynasty. Indeed the name of the county is Weichang, which means "Hunting Ground".

As it was October when we arrived at the ancient hunting ground, autumn had already set in. White birch trees stood nearly naked, save for a few yellow leaves hovering in the top branches.

Fortunately, the other trees were still bustling with life, and their thick crimson foliage set off pleasantly by the white clouds and blue sky. It was easy to imagine why this place was once chosen as a hunting ground for the most important men in China.

In *The Travels* Marco Polo had praised the stone lions on the stone railings of the Lugou Bridge. A Chinese folk saying goes "The lions on the Lugou Bridge are uncountable."

The Last Stretch of Our Journey

On a November day Marco Polo accompanied Kublai Khan on his return from the city of Shang-tu to the Great Capital in Beijing. As Marco's book failed to provide any details about this route, we decided to expedite matters by taking the highway direct to Beijing.

Continuing our southward itinerary, we found ourselves amidst mountains and overhanging cliffs. In the distance, we saw a wall wind its way along the mountain ridges. This was the second

Great Wall. It was built by Emperor Chengzu of the Ming Dynasty after he moved the capital city from the south to Beijing, for the purpose of warding off possible invasions by the Mongolians and other nomadic tribes from the north. To beef up the defenses of the new capital, he rebuilt the Great Wall, reinforced the section north of Beijing, and erected the second and third Great Walls, whose ends connected with the original Great Wall.

There are numerous mountain passes all along the way to the city of Xuanhua. The mountain town of Suoyang sits astride one of the highest mountain passages.

Like other ancient cities in China, Xuanhua is dotted with bell towers, drum towers and other buildings in the style of Ming-Dynasty architecture. In the southern part of the city we saw a Catholic church, a Gothic-looking building in distinct contrast to its surroundings. In his book Marco Polo repeatedly mentioned the fact that in China there were Buddhists, Muslims and Catholics of different denominations. It is clear that under the rulers of the Yuan Dynasty, religious activities of all kinds were tolerated.

Leaving Xuanhua we set off for our final destination, Beijing, the capital of China. The road was hemmed in between the cliffs of the rolling Yanshan Mountain Range, which was covered with green pines and trees whose leaves were just turning yellow. Shortly after we drove past Huailai County we saw a very ancient-looking town, and decided to stop to stretch our legs. A stone-tablet imbedded in the town wall was inscribed with

the name of the town – "Crowing Rooster Post Station."

In ancient times, a post station was where government couriers changed horses or stayed overnight. Local people told us that the town wall had been face-lifted for the making of a war movie. The work had been superbly done and it looked just like the real thing would have looked in its heyday. It is even possible that Marco Polo rested at this same post station as he accompanied the Great Khan on his return to the capital of Beijing.

After crossing Badaling and passing the Ming Tombs, we drove into what was once the capital of the Yuan Empire, Beijing. At a place called Hepingli not far from the Asian Games Village, we caught sight of a long ridge covered with tall trees stretching into the distance along the sparkling city moat. These were the remains of the walls of Khan-balik. In Chinese the name has been rendered as Hanbali, which means the "Great Khan's Eight Royal Compound". The magnificent structure was enclosed with a four-kilometre-long wall and deep ditches on all sides. The narrow city moat and the earth ridge overgrown with grass and trees are among the only physical reminders left today of what was the Yuan Empire, which for a time, was the largest in the world.

It was a late autumn evening when we ended our 80-day journey. We looked at our car's odometer and realized that it had taken us 12,000 kilometres, across some of China's most difficult and remote terrain. Travel – weary but happy, we felt satisfied that we had accomplished our goal. During these

Beijing *Guozijian* was first built in the 10th year of *Dade* (1306) which was the supreme learning institute of the Yuan, Ming and Qing dynasties. (Photo by Ai Liken)

two and a half months, we were taken back 700 years to one of China's most fascinating periods. The influence the great explorer Marco Polo had, not only on China but the world, should not be forgotten.

The *Da'shengshou Wan'an*
Temple White Pagoda located
in the Beijing urban area was
built in the 8th year of *Zhiyuan*
(1271) It is the earliest and
biggist extant Tibetan-style
Buddhist pagoda in China,
and had been the centre of the
Buddhist activities of the Yuan
royal family.